**A TRUE STORY OF
MIRACULOUS CHANGE AND TRANSFORMATION
AND HOW IT CAN BE YOURS**

The Ravens

SONNY PERALES

The Ravens
Copyright © 2016 Sonny Perales

All Rights Reserved. No part of this publication may be reproduced, stored in a retrieval system or transmitted in any form or by any means – electronic, mechanical, photocopy, recording or any other, except for brief quotations in printed reviews, without the prior permission of the Publisher and/or Author.

All scripture verses cited in this book come from The Holy Bible, King James Version, unless otherwise noted.

Book Cover Design: Kingdom Studios
Book Images/Newspaper Articles by Sonny Perales
Book Formatting: Douglas Fletcher
Editor: Lili Kristan

    Published by Kingdom Publishing. Kingdom Publishing is
    a registered trademark of Kingdom Studios
    KingdomStudiosNow.com

This book is also available as an eBook on Kindle.

ISBN: 13:978-0692668986
Printed in the United States of America

Foreword

by
Pastor Joel Perales

———∽———

I am Sonny's younger brother and I was too young and my parents were too naïve for us to have known anything about drugs in those days, the mid 1960's. All we knew was that my oldest brother Sonny was into something bad. He looked bad, he acted strange and his friends were weird. All we knew to do was pray. Then my dad took all my older brothers and their wives to Dallas, Texas to work on a very large freeway project. It was the construction of a major Hiway, Interstate 35, which runs North and South from the Texas border all the way to Canada. My dad had a trucking business and each one of my brothers had their own 18-wheeler truck. I started writing to Sonny and talking to him about God but I was not sure if my prayers were being heard or if Sonny was even reading my letters. I can only thank God that he did read my letters and the Holy Spirit began the work of transforming his mind and his heart at just the right time, when he needed God the most.

Later on, I enrolled in Latin American Bible Institute in La Puente, California. I came home for Christmas vacations and I was able to see Sonny during that time. The Holy Spirit quickened me to ask him for a ride back to Bible School after our holidays and to my surprise, he agreed. Little did I know was that the FBI and the narcotic undercover officers from Texas were on his trail and Sonny just wanted to get out of Texas. They had followed him from Mexico and were getting ready to move in on him when we left for California.

Later on, Sonny miraculously enrolled in the same Bible

School he brought me to. Sonny has always been very shy and still is to this day so when God called him to preach the gospel, it was yet another miracle. God had big plans for my brother. I got to see him come back to his hometown, back to skid row and bring drug addicts into his home until they got totally rehabilitated and began serving Christ.

The rest of the story is told by Sonny but I just thank God that the Lord used me to see his life changed, his family and his ministry were all transformed by the mighty power of God.

I literally saw the unsaved, the unbelievers, build his home, his church, and everything that is now SAN ANTONIO FOR CHRIST. I experienced my brother's prison ministry firsthand where he faithfully visited Texas prisons taking relatives to see their loved ones behind bars, at no cost to them. He brought Christ to those prisoners and their families and many miracles occurred because of his faithfulness and commitment.

To this day, Sonny trembles to get behind the pulpit yet the same man can lead a hardened drug addict and criminal to Christ on the streets and cast out demons without any fear whatsoever.

This book is filled with Sonny's true and inspirational life, his story is incredible and the miracles God has done through this man and his ministries are mind boggling.

If you know someone that is struggling with an addiction of any kind, I believe that this book can be the challenge and the bridge they need in coming to know Jesus as their personal and sufficient Savior.

Pastor Joel Perales
Rio de Vida Church
www.JoelandRosePerales.com
www.GospelFiesta.com

Foreword

by
Pastor Ramon Martinez

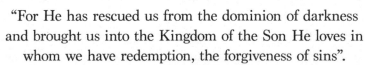

"For He has rescued us from the dominion of darkness and brought us into the Kingdom of the Son He loves in whom we have redemption, the forgiveness of sins".
Colossians 1:13-14 (NIV)

Sonny Perales' miraculous journey from a life of heroin addiction, crime and violence to becoming a Founder and the life-long Pastor of San Antonio for Christ, Inc. is yet another indisputable testimony to the supernatural power of prayer and the transforming work of Jesus and His Gospel.

"For whoever desires to save his life will lose it but whoever loses his life for My sake and the gospel's will save it."
Mark 8:35

The Perales Family and my family have been intertwined for the past sixty years. In 1970, his brother, Joel and I were students at Latin American Bible Institute located in La Puente, California. In between semesters, Joel told me that Sonny had agreed to come to Los Angeles and enroll in a drug rehabilitation program called "New House" in the city of Hacienda Heights, California. During this time, Sonny and I renewed our friendship. On one occasion, he graciously loaned me his prized car, a 1968 Mustang fastback, to drive from Los Angeles to Monterrey, California to ask for Becky's hand in marriage. We have been happily married for over forty-three years.

He successfully finished the rehab program and immediately enrolled in L.A.B.I. all within the same year. Sonny graduated from the Bible Institute and began overseeing the "New House

Rehab Ministry" in Hacienda Heights. Later that year he, his incredible wife, Lydia and children returned to San Antonio and established San Antonio For Christ Rehabilitation Home. For the past forty years, countless miracles of redemption and restoration among drug addicts and their families are the result of their ministry. This book is a real-life account of that journey and the power-packed work and amazing miracles that resulted from Sonny's decision to lose his life for the gospel's sake. Today Sonny and Lydia continue as Senior Pastors of San Antonio For Christ while their son, Michael and his wife Veronica carry this legacy to the next generation.

I can still remember Sonny's mother, Elena Perales, standing up on a fairly regular basis during our congregational time for petitions at the church we all attended growing up together and requesting that the church pray and intercede for her son, Sonny.

"Nothing of any spiritual significance happens without intercession". Oswald Chambers

Pastor Ramon H. Martinez
Founder and Senior Pastor
He Cares Ministries Inc.
San Antonio, Texas

Introduction

by
Jesse Perales
Sonny's oldest son

The Sins of the Father

I have heard it said, "Once a junkie, always a junkie"; but I have seen with my own eyes how God can truly change a man, even a junkie.

In this book, you will see what the power of God can do to so completely transform a man's life that even his own wife and children do not recognize his speech, his manner of conduct nor the faith, love and devotion that was placed into his heart. The man I am talking about is my hero, mentor, friend, confidant and also my father, Sonny Perales. Yes, he is an ex-drug addict but that is his past. When he accepted Christ into his heart as his Lord and Savior, all those addictions were broken off instantly and he became a Preacher, Teacher, Pastor, Evangelist and love in action to others bound by drugs, sins, prison and poverty. Out of his dark life came this glorious light of profound love, hope and compassion for complete strangers. His turning point was when he surrendered to Jesus Christ and the curses of the sins of my father were broken forever.

An early memory that I have of him was when I was about four or five years old. It was Christmas Eve of 1968 or 69 and I can remember hearing my mom say to me, "Go to sleep so that Santa Claus can bring you presents". It was warm and cozy in my room and I could see the Christmas tree lights down the hallway. I was awoken from my sleep when I heard my mother crying and praying out loud. Now when you are four or five years old, you really do not know what is going on, you just know that your mom is crying again; that always torn me up inside.

Long before she would start crying in prayer, I would hear music in the background. It was my Uncle Joel's music and songs. He plays the piano and sings songs from the heart. They were so anointed and they ministered to my mother during her most desperate times. They were about hope, faith, redemption and how God is greater than any of our problems. I could hear my mother pleading and crying to God asking Him to save her husband, keep him safe and bring him home that night. She would spend hours on her knees praying and crying and then she would begin to speak in other tongues, in a heavenly language. As a small boy, I did not understand it; all I knew was that mommy was crying so I would cry with her.

She would talk to God and then she would yell at the devil. I could hear her screaming at the forces of darkness saying, "You have no power over my husband", "You can't have my family".

It was about 1am and my father was not home yet. At some point my own crying would exhaust me and I would fall asleep on the floor or on the couch listening to the sounds of my mother's prayers. She would wake me up and ask me to go lay down in my bed. It was about 3 or 4am this Christmas Eve and I hear a noise in the kitchen after I had gone to my room. I looked down the hallway and I saw a shadow. My father was known to sneak in through the back door of the house. Sometimes he was gone for three or four days even up to a week; but he always came home. There were times he would sneak in and bring us some groceries, put them on top of the table or in the fridge and then leave again without saying a word to anyone.

When I heard the noise again, I slowly creped down the hallway thinking I would bump into Santa Claus. I came around very slowly with my back against the wall and I looked into the kitchen. There in the dark, I saw my father slumped over in a chair at the kitchen table with a needle still stuck in his arm and his belt wrapped around his upper arm. His legs were crossed, he was slumped over and a cigarette was in one hand. His other hand was across his knee and there was a slow blood stream coming down from his arm, dripping down to his fingertip and onto the floor.

I remember that I slowly walked over to my father and took the belt off his arm. I pulled the needle out of his vein and took the cigarette out of his hand and put them both in the sink. I got a dish cloth, rinsed it and started to wipe the blood off his arm beginning where the blood was still streaming from. After cleaning his arm and the floor, I rinsed the towel again and put it on my father's forehead. The coolness of the towel woke him up and he looked at me and smiled. He picked me up, sat me on his lap, gave me a hug and a kiss and within seconds, he dozed off again. I started playing with his hair and he woke up again. He looked straight into my eyes and just stared at me for about a minute without saying a word. Then he began to run his fingers through my hair, gave me another hug and another kiss. I knew my father loved me. He did not say it and he did not have to say it. I remember the feeling of that moment, just he and I. I felt the love that he had for me. I will never forget how he conveyed his love for me without saying a single word.

When you are that age, you don't care what your father is. He could be a drug addict, an alcoholic, a murderer, it does not matter to a child, you do not care about those things, you only care about his love. Your love at that innocent age is unconditional. All you know is that he is your father, your daddy and he loves you.

I loved my father so much that he would have to sneak out of the house to leave. If he didn't, I would wrap myself around his legs and hang on so tight and would tell him, "Please don't go daddy, please take me with you".

That night my father got up from the table and carried me to the living room. He sat me on his lap and began speaking to me in Spanish. He was caressing my hair, hugging and kissing me and playing with me. He was tickling me with the stubble on his chin and I was laughing and enjoying my father. I remember feeling so happy in his arms. As he was holding me, he lit another cigarette, inhaled a big puff of smoke, lean his head back and let the smoke out slowly. I could see the smoke coming out of his mouth. He rested his head on the back of the couch and was lying very still; I thought he was going to doze off again. I leaned my head against his chest and nuzzled in and got comfortable. He held me tighter and close to him. I was listening to his breathing and I began to doze off. His breathing was slow and steady but then in just a few minutes, it became shaky, as if he couldn't catch his breath and it stirred me up. Then he moved a little and our cheeks touched and I noticed that his were wet. When he turned, the light from the kitchen shone on his face and I could tell that he had been crying.

He sat up and put me down, gave me a final kiss and said, "Go lay down before Santa gets here". I walked down the dark hallway to my room and lay down with my head toward the door so I could watch the light from the Christmas tree. I saw him begin to cry.

I did not know what was going on or what was happening. I did not realize, as a child, the torment and pain that he was going through, caused by his addictions. He did not want to continue living that way but he did not have the willpower to get off that Ferris wheel. I can only imagine that he must have felt helpless, thinking that the only option for him was either prison or death.

I was there when my father overdosed on heroin. The fear, confusion and sadness that I felt when his friends were screaming and chaotically trying to bring him back to life was a nightmare for me. They threw him into the shower and turned cold water on him. The screams, the shaking, the crazy life and most of all the helplessness I felt because I did not know what to do. Each time I saw my parents crying, it just broke my heart.

Another vivid memory is when my mother asked me how I pretended to be daddy and I took a belt and placed it on my upper arm, like a tourniquet and then got a popsicle stick and used it to poke the veins in my arm like I saw my father doing. When she saw that, she grabbed me and said, "No, No, No, that's not how to be like daddy." She cried but I didn't know what I had done wrong. I was just doing what I saw my daddy doing.

If you are reading this book and you or someone you know has an addiction of any kind and you feel there is no way out, think again. I am here to tell you that there is definitely a way out. Jesus Christ is the Way out! Only through Him can you survive and be set free from the curse and the chains of addictions. Only Jesus can give you a new life and return joy, peace, hope, family and health back to you.

This book is a true story, I lived it and I have seen the incredible power of God to transform and completely change a life and restore a family.

I am so thankful that my father surrendered his life to Jesus Christ because without Him, my family, nor my father, would have survived.

Contents

FOREWORD .... **Joel Perales**

FOREWORD .... **Ramon Perales**

INTRODUCTION .... **Jesse Perales**

CHAPTER 1
The Black Sheep

CHAPTER 2
Running From God

CHAPTER 3
Come Home, Son

CHAPTER 4
The Life of a Drug Dealer

CHAPTER 5
The Kennedy Days

CHAPTER 6
A Vision in Hell

Contents

CHAPTER 7
Set Free and Called

CHAPTER 8
The New Home

CHAPTER 9
God Calls Me Back to San Antonio

CHAPTER 10
The Ravens

CHAPTER 11
The Miracles

CHAPTER 12
The Miracles Keep Coming

CHAPTER 13
The Bus Ministry

Contents

CHAPTER 14
Restoration Testimonies

CHAPTER 15
Lydia

CHAPTER 16
Visual Timeline

DEDICATIONS

ACKNOWLEDGEMENTS

"And it will be that you shall drink from the brook and I have commanded the ravens to feed you there." So he (Elijah) went and did according to the word of the Lord, for he went and stayed by the Brook Cherith, which flows into the Jordan. The ravens brought him bread and meat in the morning and bread and meat in the evening and he drank from the brook.
1 Kings 17:4-6

CHAPTER ONE

The Black Sheep

I WAS RAISED A CHRISTIAN in a Spanish Pentecostal Church and almost all my family were Christians. I had relatives who were ministers, pastors and evangelists. All of my mother's grandchildren serve God in some kind of ministry. My uncles were ministers and that was all I knew, the Christian life. My parents taught me about God but I only knew religion, I did not have a relationship with God and I wasn't save, I had not accepted Jesus Christ as my personal Savior. Everybody thought I was saved because I came from a Christian home but as I grew up, I became so rebellious that pretty soon it was obvious that I wasn't saved at all. The church was shocked when they found out that I was the black sheep. I had started drinking and smoking and rebelled more and more against the way I was raised. I got into fights inside the church and had trouble with authority. No one could make me obey. I grew up thinking like those of the world. I went after young girls my age and took marijuana to church to sell. I loved money and the things that it buys all those worldly things. Everywhere I went, I smoked and sold marijuana. Finally, they ran me off the church property because of my bad behavior. The Christian people could no longer tolerate me and they did not want me around. I was told to leave. They condemned me and would not forgive me. Many times I would fight inside the church building. Once I chased another young boy right inside to the altar. That day, the church leaders asked me to leave. After that, I would never come close to a church. I was fourteen years old at this time.

I was also having trouble in school; problems just seemed to follow me. I started having more and more trouble with authority figures, the police, school teachers and principals, my pastor, my mother and father. I then started a gang in my neighborhood. We called ourselves the Ghost Tower Gang. During 1951, I lived in the barrio around 19th and Tampico Streets and there were very few schools for Mexicans. There were only two schools at the time, Lanier and Tech High Schools. We could not get into Lanier because it was full so we were sent to Tech but Tech High School had the teens from Casiano Courts, Ghost Town, Lake 24th Street, Las Colonias and Las Palmas Barrios but the gangs were closer to downtown, which was where Tech High School was.

In 1951, I went to Tech High School and the very first day, we clashed with our rival gang. A gang war broke out right in front of the Tech High School office. We were sent home and never even made it inside the school building. The police chased us and caught some of us. The second day we showed up more prepared with knives and chains but the police were ready too. There were policemen everywhere. That second day, they caught more of us and warned us that if we showed up again, they would send us to juvenile correction. Eventually the School also told me to leave and I was expelled from Tech High School when I was not even register. I came back two or three days later and was told not to hang around. Officially, I was never expelled since I was never registered in the school but my father received a letter thanking him for not sending me to that school. After that, I was in the streets but I always had a desire to make money because my father was a business man and even though I was only fourteen, I had dreams of being rich. My father did not want me to be hanging out in the streets, he wanted me to be educated but I couldn't because I knew that due to gang violence, I could be thrown into jail. My father and I fought all the time, he would force me to go to school but I would not go. Instead, I would pretend to go and just stay out all day long so my parents thought I was in school during the day. When my father found out, I left home because he also found out that I was using drugs and I did not want to hurt him, so I left the house.

After the incident at Tech High School, I graduated to using heroin. At first I started using one time only and then the following week, maybe twice that week and then I was using once a day and then it grew to two, three and four injections per day. That was just to be normal and have a normal day. I guess what bothered me most was that I knew I came from a good family. I saw the pain in my mother's eyes. I ran into her in the streets and she would ask for my forgiveness because she didn't know what she had done wrong to cause me to leave the family and use drugs. She came from a decent family and it was a shameful thing to have a drug addict in the family. I knew that I greatly offended my family not just because they loved me so much but because of their Christian beliefs.

In those days, it was not true Christianity, it was religiosity and very legalistic. My sins were considered a curse. By the time I was fifteen, I was lost and nobody wanted me. When I would go visit my friends, their parents would run me off. They would chase me off their properties with a broom.

Today addiction is not looked down as a curse or a sin, now it is looked on as an illness. They even give you free needles so you won't get AIDS and you don't spread it. But in the early 50's, if they found a needle in your possession or in your backyard, they would give you thirty years in prison. If you hid an addict from the law in your house, it was against the law. The law has changed since then. At that time, they did not know why people injected themselves with such deadly drugs.

So, young and wild, I left for Chicago with my cousin. We stole a car and went as far as La Mesa, Texas. We had no idea how to get to Chicago; we just knew that it was north so we went north. We were so stupid; we did not even know where Chicago was so we got to La Mesa in December completely unprepared for the trip. We were wearing nylon shirts in the middle of winter, freezing with no money and no gas. We quickly had no food to eat so we stopped at a gas station and a man offered us a job pitching bales of cotton. He paid us fifty cents which was just enough to buy gas to go to his ranch. We had not eaten so he gave us another fifty cents so we could buy some bread and Spanish peanuts and we made ourselves some burritos. We were so hungry. The next day, we worked hard on the Ranch. We slept in the car with no blankets and it was freezing. All we had were the nylon shirts with short sleeves and it was snowing outside. The man did not offer us anything warm. That afternoon, he paid us fifty cents an hour, which gave us enough money to go back to San Antonio and start all over again.

When we got back, we found out that the man who owned the car we had stolen was watching us and found the car right away once we got into San Antonio. He took his car back. A friend of ours stole another car for us because he wanted to go to Chicago with us so finally we started for Chicago again. This time we were a little more prepared, we took jackets and blankets and this time we had more money, enough for the trip.

I was fifteen years old and was not afraid of anything. My cousin's father lived in Chicago except that we did not have an address for him. We just knew that he was a wino and lived in the downtown area of Chicago where all the winos hang out. When we arrived in Chicago the first night, we slept in the car. We were told to search down Halstead and Madison Streets. The car broke down and we could not get it started. Chicago never slept; it was wide open at all hours of the night, the bars, stores and night life. In the morning, we went to eat at the local wino hangout and ran right into my uncle. I actually had two uncles there, one was my mother's brother and the other was married to my mother's sister. One was named Tony and the other Polo. When they saw us, they were very surprised. We were so young but Uncle Tony was happy to see his son who had traveled with us from San Antonio. He was happy but still got very angry with me for bringing his son on such a long and difficult trip. They were hung over but even so, he took his belt and started waving it at me and saying, "You are not this kind of person, you come from a Christian family. You shouldn't be here!"

They accepted me because I lied and gave them a sad story about my father. I told them that he abused me, beat me, made me work and took all my money. They felt sorry for me, so they kept me with them. They were homeless and lived in an abandoned building with no bathtub. They stayed warm by putting firewood and just broken pieces into a fifty-five gallon drum and lighting it on fire. That was their heat source during those brutal Chicago winters. My uncles begged for money so they could buy their wine but we were too proud, instead we stole. After a while, my uncles really liked us because we bought their wine. We started to steal from stores until my cousin started purse snatching and found there was more money in that. My cousin, Mike, stole one purse per day, as needed, until we started getting good at it and then we would work two or three together. We had a system worked out and stole purses for about six months. Chicago was bad, nobody cared to get involved. We finally were able to get an upstairs apartment and my uncles were happy because now we could take baths.

My friend, Jimmy, made a connection for marijuana so we started selling. We did not have to steal anymore. The landlady also owned The San Antonio Bar and we would keep an eye on the bar for her so she did not charge us rent. We did odd jobs and overall did what we wanted. The landlady liked us, she always had her eye on me and maybe she liked me because I worked hard. If she needed a bouncer, we were handy so she called us for help. I would also fix her car. I know now that God was in control of my life even then because He would send people to help take care of us. We always had money in our pockets. She would always slip me a twenty here and there.

We were at The San Antonio Bar for over a year and my mother and father didn't know where I was all this time. Nobody from San Antonio knew I was in Chicago. I suffered in Chicago because there was a loneliness and sadness inside of me. I missed my family and loved them very much yet I knew I couldn't live a Christian life. I just did not fit into their life. I would embarrass them so I really did not want to be there. I felt like I did not fit in at all. I had food, lodging and money so for now, I was okay. I believe the Lord used the landlady to help care for me like a mother. It was some kind of a home. We would talk and I would do errands for her. I never charged her yet she would always pay me. The bar was always full, even though it was a dangerous place; God gave me a place to live. It was hard to rent an apartment at age fifteen, but God made it possible. I had money for clothes, I was always clean and now I know that it was God's hand of grace and protection upon me all those years. The landlady would ask me if I needed anything such as ironing, even though she knew we were thieves and sold drugs. She still trusted me behind the bar, where she had a lot of money in her cash register.

Finally someone told my father that I was in Chicago and instinctively, he knew exactly where I was. He came to Chicago and to take me home. We had a long talk. I told him I did not want to embarrass them but my father said that it did not matter for me to come home anyway. He was crying because I did not want to go with him. I just didn't want to hurt them or make them a laughing stock because of me. He said, "I will put you to work in my business."

While I was in Chicago, I would spend the day at Ocean Drive and would sometimes see the Army recruiting officer. But when I tried to enlist, the recruiting officer laughed and said, "You're only sixteen years old and you only weigh 108 pound, go home!" I told my father that I wanted to enlist in the Army. His response was "No, you'll get killed!" Once we got back to San Antonio, I tried enlisting in the Military again but this time in the Navy. They rejected me because of my age and weight again. On my way, I saw the Army Air Corp and walked into their office and said I want to enlist. They said, "Yes, but you need to bring your father and he has to sign." I told my Father and after much discussion about it, he agreed to sign for me since he knew that I would go back to Chicago if he did not help me enlist.

I signed up for active duty in 1952 for a total of four years. I took my basic training and most of all I wanted to go to the frontline. I wanted to see Korea and Japan. I wanted to see the world. I had plans and dreams to go to war. I was very young and did not use my head but God had other plans. When I finished basic training at Lackland in San Antonio, Texas, I realized that I was right back where I started, in my home town again. I felt like I was just moving in circles when all I wanted was to see the world. Kelly Field proved to be good to me. The Army Air Corp sent me to school and I was able to get my G.E.D. Soon it was 1956 and the war had ended but I had gotten worse, my behavior had not improved. I had picked up even more vices.

My purpose for joining the Military was to go to war. Everyone else was afraid but not me. I wanted to fight, I wanted to travel. I didn't think about loyalty to my country, just getting out and doing what I wanted. The recruiter told me I would see war and that I would see the world. No one at the Lackland Training Center wanted to go because men were getting killed. The training officer would tell us you have two months then he would say, you have one month, he wanted to make sure we were trained right so we could defend ourselves. Every time I talked to my buddies, they would tell me I was crazy because I wanted to go to war. In my squadron there were more than 300 men and only one third made it through the training. They were either too fat, had heart problems or just didn't pass. Some would faint and the ambulances would come pick them and they were never seen again. Graduation Day was Beer Party Day, everyone was crying with their buddy. We had developed friendships and we knew we might never see each other again. The Drill Instructor gave us his blessing saying, "may God have mercy on all of you." After that all night party, many were passed out. It was a time of love and unity even though we only knew each other for three months. We hugged each other and held each other like little kids because we knew that many would not make it back.

The next day, the Sergeant came with orders for everyone which included a 15 day furlough. He started calling out names, everyone got their orders except me. I was left alone in the barracks. I did not know what was happening. A couple of days later, I found out. The Commanding Officer called me to his office and asked me, "What are you doing here, son?" I thought to myself, "Don't you know?" He continued, "you are too young, you should be in school. I am not going to send you to Korea." I felt bad, I really wanted to go and I told him so. He said, "No one wants to go to war, what is the matter with you? Are you crazy?" He began checking my records and saw the name of my recruiting officer and said, "I am going to have a talk with your recruiting officer, you should not be here." But all I could say was, "I want to go to war!" He said, "No, if I send you; you will get killed for sure, you are just a kid!" I replied by saying, "No, I am a man!" I wanted to tell him that I had been around, I had gone to Chicago on my own and taken care of myself but I didn't. He said, "Look, son, you think you know what is best but I am going to send you to school." I answered, "But if you send me to school, my friends will find out and I told them that I was going to war." He just smiled at me and said, "You are going to school and since you have enlisted, you have to obey." He killed my spirit. That wasn't my plan but God had other plans for me.

When he saw that I got angry he said that after I get my G.E.D., he would re-consider sending me to Korea and that I had a good spirit because I wanted to fight for my country. He thought I wanted to fight but I just wanted to see the world and have a good time. He said that I needed time to grow up first so I was off to school. It took nine months for me to get my G.E.D. but first he gave me a 15 day furlough.

My mother thought I was going to Korea so when I got home with my duffel bag and in my uniform, everyone was expecting me to go to Korea so everyone was very sad. I was angry, I threw my cap on the floor and mom asked me, "Why are you angry?" I told her that it didn't matter at all that I had enlisted. I am not going to Korea! My mom jumped up all excited. She was so happy

The Black Sheep

and everyone was hugging me. They called Pastor Manuel De La Cruz and everyone came over and they had a worship service at the house. My mom was singing along with the other sisters of the church who had been praying and fasting for me not to go to war. Mom told me that an evangelist had told her two weeks ago that she did not have to worry about her son because her petition before heaven had been answered.

The church had many men who were drafted and had been killed already so people were really worried about me enlisting. When mom told me about that, I got even madder. I left the house before the Pastor got there. I enlisted and then my family and these church people were praying against what I wanted the most, boy was I angry! God had answered their prayers. I stayed away for three days. At night I would go the military base and stay in the barracks by myself. I was too angry to go home. When my furlough was over, I went back to school. I could go home on weekends but I did not, I stayed in the barracks. My parents would come and take me home sometimes.

I had a graduation ceremony and I received a diploma. I would stay in the barracks anxiously waiting for my orders. Even though the war had ended, many didn't know it was over and some said the war continued in caves. Nobody came with my orders so I went to the Commanding Officer's office with my diploma in hand to show him. You just do not go knock on your Commanding Officer's door without an appointment or being called there but I did. I knocked and he said, "Come in." He liked my salute. I walked in and showed him my paperwork on the school graduation. He told me he was proud of me because I had obeyed his orders. I told him I wanted him to know that I was ready for Korea. He started to laugh and told me that the war was over and that the fighting had stopped. The United States had signed a treaty with them. Then he said, "Let me congratulate you." He got up from his chair and walked around his desk and extended his hand to me. We shook hands. He then said that he had another school in El Paso, Texas that he wanted me to attend and that it was for top secret training. They had done my security clearance while I was in school at Lackland.

I was transferred to El Paso. The C.O. told me that the Military Police Training would be harder than the basic training. I was there for three months. We had camouflage, biking, marches with field packs and went on long hikes. When I finished military police training, I was sent to top secret training where I was taught about airplane operations, how the airplanes are sabotaged due to Korean and Chinese terrorists breaking in and blowing up the airplanes. The school trained us to inspect the B-52 and B-36 planes. Korea was afraid of these bomber planes because they could fly very low or very high and were able to drop bombs from these heights. When the training was over, I was told that I was not going to Korea so I march right up to my Commanding Officer in El Paso and explained to him that the C.O. in San Antonio had told me that I was going to Korea after this training. He said, "I am your C.O. now, no one else and we are not sending anyone to Korea, we are withdrawing men from Korea." I got even angrier. I told him I would request a transfer.

From the military police in El Paso, I was transferred to Durant, Oklahoma and I went right into the motor pool so I could drive a truck. At Durant, after they had seen my papers, the Sergeant asked me, "What are you doing here? You had a very good job in El Paso. You were in the military police, that is a clean job and you get to wear good looking uniforms, here you are going to wear fatigues." I didn't care, I was happy there. I stayed in the motor pool for about two and a half years. Even though I was happy there, I still wanted more. I was never truly happy. I had other ideas.

CHAPTER TWO

Running From God

SINCE MY YOUTH, I knew God wanted me, but I kept running. I knew in my inner spirit that there was a call on my life. You are never happy when you run away from God, you never have peace. The C.O. wanted the best for me, he saw my potential but I was stubborn. The Military Police was a good place for me but my rebellious spirit would not leave me alone. I knew they were right but since I was running from God, I had no peace.

When you run from God you are never happy and there is a kind of fear inside of you. I was never saved but yet something bothered me. Almost every night I would pray but I did not like Christian people so I fought against being a Christian myself. I would go to church once in a while just to please my mother. I really did not want drugs but I did not want the Christina life either. Inside of me I knew that I had some kind of calling on my life but I did not want it. Some people have had a bad experience with Christianity so they reject God altogether. After the motor pool, I was discharged from the Army. The last year of my service I saw the soldiers coming home from Korea and they had become addicted to opium or heroin. Opium is like gum; it can also be injected or smoked but heroin is mostly injected with a needle. The soldiers arrived and stayed at the barracks while many were hooked on heroin, I was a drunk and a pill heard and once in a while I would get a fix.

What the North Koreans did, as part of their war strategy, was to give the soldiers free heroin to get them addicted to it when they were on furloughs. Prostitution was rampant and the women would give the soldiers the heroin and the girls would bring the heroin into the army camp. That was part of the war plan in Korea. The women would come into the fox holes with drugs. The military knew about it but did not know how bad the problem was. The US may have thought that if the young soldiers used heroin, they may be able to fight without fear. The soldiers got hooked and stayed in Korea for a year; they were no good to anyone. During the Vietnam War, the drug they used was L.S.D. Soldiers came back from Korea and many brought back contraband, some were loaded with drugs. The Koreans had a very good strategy because fear caused many of the soldiers to take the drug. In the Vietnam War, the drugs were hallucinating, where heroin hurts your body, not your mind but L.S.D. hurts your mind.

The problem started in 1953, many of the Koreans did not know the war had ended and many soldiers stayed behind to do military clean up. Of those who stayed to clean up, many came back hooked. The drugs eventually ran out and they had to start making connections. Felipe Mercado, who got hooked in Korea, came back and he was assigned to my barracks. Prior to my release, we became friends. We were stationed in Sherman, Texas which is where I got my final discharge. We were there one year. The junkie soldiers didn't have a place to buy their drugs so when Felipe arrived he asked me if I knew of a connection. We were stationed in a dry county so I had been selling beer from the army base. We realized we had a good market since Sherman was a small town. Dallas was the nearest and largest city but there they only had drug store addicts, prescription addicts, which they received from their corrupt doctors. We really didn't know Dallas very well so we decided to go to San Antonio. We started making purchases in San Antonio and Laredo and then we would transport the drugs to Sherman. A friend of mine had a house which became a drug connection and our customers were the soldiers. By this time, it was 1956 and this is when I became a regular user of heroin. I had been a volunteer on base after my discharge since I didn't want to re-enlist. I was hooked so I wasn't right, my behavior was suspicious and the police started to pay attention because burglaries had gone up in the area. The soldiers had started to steal to support their drug habit. They had not really wised up to the drugs until crimes went up so drastically.

We always got our fix in the house never on the army base. One day, just as I was getting ready to be discharged, a group of us decided to go downtown. There was a revival tent near Interstate 45; revivals were a familiar site in those days. Tent services were more common than churches. It was about 8:00pm. The revival service had started around 6pm. We had to make a left turn but there at the blinking light, Felipe said, "Turn left - no right". He had noticed the tent revival and some of the girls were dancing in the spirit. He did not know what that meant, but I did. All he knew was that there was music, dancing and girls and he was interested. We could hear them from miles away and when we got there, the guys were anxious to see what was going on. I was walking very slowly because I knew it was a revival service. I told them, "Don't go in, let's go back, let's stay in the back." We had been there a while when the music stopped. I told them, "these are the Hallelujahs, let's get out of here." But they said, "Look at those girls, when this is all over, they are going to need a ride." Sherman had no Mexican population and the town's residents treated us alright. The girls were Christian but they were also looking our way and smiling. I was uncomfortable and sweating even though it was Fall. I did not want this; I told my friend that I was leaving. They were already high on drugs and didn't realize where they were. The evangelist stopped preaching and called me to the front but I told the others, "It's you he wants." I started backing away but another man stopped me. He said, "Don't go, God wants to talk to you", but I didn't want God to talk to me. I didn't want that life; I did not want to be a hypocrite. That is what I thought Christians were, hypocrites, legalistic, religious but I never felt their love, I had only felt their judgment and condemnation. I was happy the way I was, I could hear the man talking to me but I kept thinking he is just going to embarrass me and point out my faults in front of everybody. But he was different, he told me that God loved me and that I was somebody special to God. He told me I was running from God because I had a wrong concept of God but that God was showing him that God had a big work planned for me. He said I was in danger but that God was always with me. He wanted me to know God was with me. He told me that he saw me on a long road and that I would have a long life and that he saw me with a white robe down that road. God will let you live your life until you are ready for Him, he said. He is going to let you taste that life. It is a long road but you are His and He will be with you until you are ready to serve Him.

When I left that night, I was not happy at all. I should have been happy when I received that word of knowledge but I wasn't ready for it. Shortly after that, Felipe got caught with drugs and was given a dishonorable discharge. I went to court with him and the lawyer's defense was that the military should take into consideration the North Korean's strategy of providing drugs for the soldiers. The United States may have won that war but the men lost their families and many their lives due to the fact that drugs were so easy to obtain and in many case, only at arm's reach to soldiers. That is why so many came home addicted to drugs, mostly heroin. Felipe had just married and had a new baby when he was discharged. With a dishonorable discharge nobody would hire him. The lawyer pointed out that he had fought for his country and that he fell into the Koreans trap. Felipe was a casualty of war and now was a disgrace to his family. Felipe would become an outcast to society. Drug addiction was unheard of in 1956; there were no programs to help rehabilitate Felipe.

The lawyer kept pleading for Felipe, he needs help, he kept saying. Is this country going to turn their back on him? Instead of helping him, he was given a dishonorable discharge. What is he going to do with his wife and child? What is he going to do on the streets, no one will hire him, he needs our help. Felipe was still hooked and the answer was not to put him on the streets, he needed medical attention.

The Gulf War of 1992 resulted in casualties because of chemical warfare. Saddam Hussein used the same strategy that the North Koreans used in using drugs. There was no difference because they used chemicals, the only difference was the kind of drug used and how it was administered. The difference with the soldiers was that the Gulf War casualties were given their benefits. The Korean War casualties lost their benefits, self-respect and careers because the government did not acknowledge the strategy the Koreans used. Similar to the Gulf War when their wives got pregnant, because of the chemicals used, their babies were born deformed. The Korean veterans who came back addicted to heroin, since they were not aware of the problem of the drug addiction passing on to the unborn child through the blood, their babies were born addicted to the drug and consequently died because they did not know how to treat them for the addiction. Felipe was only one of the casualties, imagine these by the thousands. The government took their benefits away and they went home to their wives and made junkies out of them. That was the Korean plan to weaken America and from then on drug abuse has increased. After Felipe got dishonorably discharged, he came to San Antonio and was killed during a robbery break-in. I believe that the government killed him because they could not help him fight the drug addiction. They had no rehabilitation programs to offer him and others like him. All they did, at that time, was to pass laws against drugs and the use of drugs.

Although the military knew that the Korean prostitutes were bringing the soldiers drugs, they allowed it because it took away the soldiers fear since heroin takes away all feeling. Why didn't the military do shake downs or raids in the army barracks? Why? Because they knew the drugs were there, they knew they were getting them for free but it never came into their mind that it was a war strategy. The U.S. military liked it that their men became fearless. They allowed this in Korea but as soon as the soldiers came back, they received a dishonorable discharge. They lost all their benefits and were called "turn coats". They never received a hero's welcome.

When Felipe left, my eyes were wide awake to this injustice. I was about to be discharged myself and I knew the police were getting wiser to the illegal activities we were conducting because they had started doing surveillance. I did not want to get caught so I decided not to re-enlist. I would have needed to re-enlist for six more years and by that time Cambodia was acting up and I did not want to see the world anymore. Felipe and others had told me their war stories and I realized that I did not want any part of it. When I saw how the soldiers were coming home injured, addicted and how they were being treated by the government, I knew I did not want to re-enlist again. I applied for an early out, because of the surveillance that I was now under and was released about three months early.

The soldiers did not know what to do about their addictions, some went to doctors who gave them prescriptions for pain killers and others became social cast outs, people, family and friends all turned against them. After a time, the military snapped and they realized that the veterans were coming back hooked on these deadly drugs and they began to establish programs to help them. Maybe the government realized what had happened but they never admitted it publicly or else they would have had to give the Vets back all their benefits and back pay. To this day, many Korean War Vets are trying to get reinstated to receive benefits by reversing their dishonorable discharge. It has been over forty-five years now and that mistreatment has never been corrected.

After I got out of the service, I went to Chicago much wiser and older and this time I took plenty of winter clothes. A friend of mine who was in the Army with me, an Italian boy named Shi, had given me his phone number and he lived in Chicago so I looked him up and stayed with him for a week. During our liberty, while in the Army, I had taken him to San Antonio with me and he met one of my sisters so when I stayed with him, he introduced me to one of his sisters. She was nice and we became friends but I had no romantic inclinations for her at all. She had a large Italian nose and was too tall for me. The Italians like to drink everyday so I began my daily drinking habit. One day I was introduced to his uncle who worked at the Soo-Line railroad and Shi and I were able to get jobs there. We were excited; this job paid us $3.18 per hour while in San Antonio this work would have been a $.50 per hour job.

They had a lot of wetbacks so it was easy to become a crew leader right away. I went on drinking very day, although I backed off drugs. I had a cousin who was a drug addict but I tried not to hang around with him very much. The railroad gave us apartments and we had a restaurant at the terminal. They had a lot of work for us so we could work two shifts if we wanted to. We worked as a freight handler during the day and at night we worked in the terminal. It snowed so much during winter in Chicago so we swept the tracks or switched the boxcars constantly. We received a lot of overtime and double time. The apartments that the railroad gave us were located in the railroad yard. They were shared rooms and we did not have to cook but they were full of wetbacks, young boys and men from Mexico who did not have their legal papers to be in the United States. They had come over just to work to take care of their families or to build their dreams. Their English was very limited, some did not speak English at all and they were very poorly educated, most could not read or write.

The first day of work, Shi went home after work but I stayed in the railroad camp. We had showers and heaters. I got my bed and on my first night I discovered that my roommate happened to be a Christian. We started to talk about God. Here we go again, I thought to myself. I left San Antonio to get away from Christianity and yet here it is right next to me once more. I could not get away from it, it seemed. It was always following me and showing up everywhere I went. This guy would pray every night and he would pray for me as well. He told me that he knew that God was going to use me one day. I wondered in my heart, "How does he know God is going to use me?" I did not want anything to do with that kind of life... why don't they just leave me alone?

I worked for the railroad in Chicago for three years. The pay was really good but I drank every single day. I would not work on Sundays because I lied to my employer and told them that it was against my religion to work on Sundays. So they never scheduled me on Sundays. I would go downtown and just fool around. My roommate would work on Sundays because he was saving money to build a church in Mexico. When he left, I rested for a while but not for long, I got another roommate and he was a Christian too. I knew it was my mother's faithful prayers to God that were constantly interceding for me and bringing God and good Christians to surround me so that I would be constantly hearing the word of God and covered by prayer.

CHAPTER THREE

Come Home, Son

ONE DAY IN 1958, my father came down with tuberculosis, a very contagious disease that demanded the patients be quarantined. My father coughed all night. At the same time, my mother was pregnant with my little brother, Abel, who was infected with tuberculosis in the womb. Abel got TB in the womb through the blood and he was born with it. His condition was actually worse than my father's because Abel had no immunity built up. The doctors in San Antonio found out about Abel's case. The family was very upset and they knew this would be very hard because when you had TB back in the late 50's, they quarantined you from the rest of your family because it was so contagious and they had no way of controlling the spread of disease at that time. So when this was discovered by the doctors, they sent the police to my family's house. That was the law in those days. The authorities came to decontaminate the house, cooking utilities and my father's bed and bathroom. Afterwards they took everyone to the hospital to check them for TB. I was still in Chicago and they knew that because of my recent military service, I must be in good health because every soldier undergoes extensive vaccinations and must be in good physical health.

My father called me and asked me to come home. He wanted

me to come home to help him run his trucking business and help take care of the family since he was very sick. The family had known that I was in Chicago and how to find me.

Instead of going home, I suggested they come to Chicago for a visit because there was a hospital in Grand Rapids, Michigan, that was testing a new drug for TB and they were looking for people infected with the disease to test their drug on them. This was better news for them than not having any options of survival for my father or Abel in San Antonio. My family had the money to make the trip so they decided to come. My father was admitted quickly because this was a totally new and experimental drug testing and they needed guinea pigs. At this time, I had a brand new 1957 car so I was able to drive mom to apply at the hospital and my father was admitted right away.

I went back to work at Soo-Line Railroad and every week I would go see my father. When we left him there, the doctors informed us that tuberculosis was very contagious and that they had no cure at that time. He did not give us any hope but my mother told him that we were Christians and that many were praying for my father's healing. The doctor said, "Only God can save him." They were experimenting with those that had tuberculosis; my father was given new experimental drugs. While we were waiting to see how my father would react to the drugs and treatments they were giving him, we saw a family crying because their father had just died of TB. He was all covered up when the ambulance came to get him.

We began to make plans to move the family from San Antonio to Chicago where we could easily visit my father in Grand Rapids. We rented a house in Chicago to stay near my father. The family business had received a contract from the Unemployment Office transporting workers to Kokomo, Indiana. The migrant workers were Mexican and Jamaicans who worked in the tomato, strawberry and cherry fields. The contract also included transporting produce to Traverse City, Michigan and then to Chicago so it was a very good contact. I got real involved in working for them but my father didn't want me to work, he wanted me to keep watch

Come Home, Son

over the family.

After Traverse City, came Ludington where we came for the onions, cucumber fields and we followed the crops. We stayed in Chicago and the family trucking business went to North Dakota to the potato crop then the sugar beets and then transported to the canneries. By the following year, the trucking business went back to San Antonio.

My father was put in a semi-private room. There were a total of fifty patients in that hospital which was more like a private nursing home than a regular hospital. It was very nice. The man that was in the room next to my father was a Mexican national. The next week we came to visit and we found out that he had died. We lived with anxiety and frustration all the time; wanting to do something more but couldn't. It was amazing to me that throughout this ordeal my mother's faith kept her going. One day the hospital found out about Abel's serious illness and the police was called in. They wanted to take Abel from my mother. He was only one-year-old at this time. My mother said, "No". "I would prefer you kill me, she said, I will not give this baby up". They said, "We will lock you up, that baby is contagious." She replied, "Go ahead and lock me up or kill me but I won't give him up." The police kept saying you will get TB yourself. They could not understand why she did not have TB already; it was a mystery. I thought to myself, if the baby was inside of her and he got TB, why didn't my mother get TB since it travels through the blood. I couldn't understand it either. She should have had the disease but she didn't. She told me, "I don't have TB because I serve God."

Before my family moved to Chicago, the police in San Antonio also tried to take the baby by force when they found out that Abel was contagious. My mother would begin calling out scripture to the police officers, healing scriptures. The rest of the family, my little brothers and sisters, would get involved too. They would begin pulling on the officers' pants, kicking them and trying to get them away from my mother and the baby. Because they were all underage, the police could not restrain them so they went to the judge to get a court order. We will be back and take everyone to jail, they would say as they were leaving the house. We will bring the wagon for all of you, they exclaimed. So what mom did was to hide, just like when Moses was a baby and his mother took and hid him, my mother took and hid Abel. When the police came back with the warrant they could not find her. Mom hid for a while, in the meantime, my father still ran the business quarantined from the rest of the family in the house in San Antonio. Mom was hiding with the baby, who knows where. Right about that time is when we discovered the hospital in Grand Rapids so the family moved from San Antonio to Chicago.

When they arrived in Grand Rapids, they had to keep Abel's illness a secret because nobody wanted to rent to them if they knew someone in the family had TB. It was like having AIDS back in the 80's, people were afraid and there was no cure for it. So it was for tuberculosis in the 50's, it was a very frightening disease. No one especially the hospital was to know about Abel or they would take him away from us. The authorities would take the babies with tuberculosis and eventually the babies would die because there was no cure and their mothers and the entire family would suffer for that death. The doctors in San Antonio told my mother not to kiss Abel because the disease would spread to her but mom ignored that, she hugged and kissed my little brother all the time. He was her youngest and she did not care about catching the deadly disease, she had faith. She would visit my father and leave Abel behind because he would cough constantly and that was a dead giveaway. She would say, "Chinto, see why we are suffering it's because of you, because you were a womanizer and a drunk. It is time for you to repent and give your life to Christ." On one of the visits, just about a month after he was put in the Grand Rapids hospital, my father gave his life to Christ and received salvation. He said he had a vision near the ponds behind the hospital. I know my father really had a supernatural experience with God because he had always been a hard man, never spoke much about his emotions and never about God. But after only four months, he starting talking about the Lord and sharing his vision with us. We noticed the difference in him immediately because patients with tuberculosis had no strength and that day my father was sitting up in the recliner in his room and his face looked very happy, with a big smile. Before that time, he was sad and in pain, now he was laughing, joking and joy showed on his face. He said excitedly, "Let me tell you what happened!" He got up and asked me for forgiveness and he was not the type to ask for forgiveness. He said he was grateful because I had been looking out for the family and all their needs. The house payments were made, there was plenty of food, we never lost anything and we were never in need. My mother always paid her tithes and gave offerings. That day we all noticed that things begin to change more rapidly in my father's physical condition as well as his spiritual life.

We left the hospital and went back to Chicago but came back in two weeks. The hospital was really beautiful; they provided guest houses where the patient's family could stay when they came for a visit. We would stay Friday night and Saturday but this particular Friday, the doctor left us a note. He wanted us to stop by his office; he had something important to say to us. I was a little bit anxious because it said that it was an emergency. Mom said, "It's not bad news, he is going to tell us that your father is healed." Tell the Doctor we will be here all day Saturday so we can see him any time. We had a telephone in our guest house and we got a call from the doctor, he wanted a meeting with us. When we got there, he showed us my father's x-rays and he had a big smile on his face. In the very first examination, when my father first arrived at the hospital, there were several holes in his lungs, the doctor showed us the first x-rays and then he showed us the last x-rays taken. They took weekly x-rays to monitor the patients taking the experimental drugs. The current x-rays showed my father's lungs were perfectly normal, no holes at all. The doctor was very excited. There should be scars, he said, but there are no scars at all. He could not figure it out; eventually he had to admit that it was a supernatural healing. It was my mother's faith filled prayers. God answered her prayers and the prayers of many others that were praying for my father's healing. Father had no more tuberculosis. The doctor wanted my father to stay so that the medical teams could test him; they wanted to know if this was a direct result of the medicines they used or if something else had occurred. They wanted to test his salvia and to find out if the TB germ was still present in his body. They were elated but still wanted to run many more tests. They also wanted to monitor for signs of the TB coming back but most of all they wanted to know if they had discovered the drug effective on TB. Did they have a breakthrough with their testing?

My father really wanted to tell anyone who would listen about God's love and his healing and the doctor truly wanted to know so they spoke a lot about it together. My father said, "I gave my life to Jesus and I know He has healed me. When I was at the pond, He told me that He was going to heal me." The doctor stopped him there and said, "I can't write that in your medical reports." My mother said to the doctor, "You are a very educated man but you don't believe in miracles?" The doctor replied, "You mean everyone here can get healed?" Mom said, "Yes, if they believe." The doctor did not want to hear the rest; he just shook his head in disbelief. My father stayed for the next three months but one day he called me to come and pick him up, he was ready to leave for good. On our drive out, he could not stop talking about God. He had a shopping bag full of medicines given to him by the doctors at the hospital and suddenly he told me to stop at the bridge. He took the bag full of medicines, pills and needles, medicines that the doctors told him he had to continue taking otherwise the TB might return and he left them at the bridge. He said, "How can I continue to be a witness of the power of God and still use these medicines?" I begged him not to leave them but he was convinced of his total healing and that he did not need to take any pills at all. He never had a sick day after that, he never kept another appointment and he never had any more coughs. He was miraculously healed by God.

Father and I arrived back in Chicago where mom and Abel and the rest of the family were. Abel was still sick and the doctors said that my father could get sick again but he was full of faith so he picked Abel up and kissed and hugged him. He did not care about getting sick again, he knew that God was with him. After my father was healed, he started missing San Antonio, the city was his home and it was always in his heart but Abel had been our immediate problem, so they couldn't go back yet. We never got use to the cold winters in Chicago, everyone wanted to go back to San Antonio's warm weather.

My mother said, "You go, I am staying here with Abel". One of my aunts lived close by and after a few months, she talked my mother into taking Abel to the hospital. Mom was a prayer warrior and did not normally go to hospitals or doctors. I constantly encouraged her to go so one cold, snowy day, she finally agreed. It was below zero outside that night and after warming up the car, everyone bundled up and we headed to the hospital. Even father insisted on coming, he was not going to stay behind. The hospital was fifteen miles away, near Franklin Park and we had every intention of getting there even with the extreme freezing weather against us. It was a Sunday night and we were out in the country and we came across a small church with a steeple, looked more like a "Little House on the Prairie". There was a revival sign that said 'healings in Jesus' name'. When my father saw it he got all excited and said, "Stop here!" I said, "No, we need to get to the hospital or Abel will die and you want to go to church?" Dad said, "Sonny, look what it says, "Healings", that is what we want, a healing for Abel."

My father had truly changed his faith; it was now like my mother's strong faith. In his suffering, God had touched his life and transformed him so completely. So I pulled over and they went inside the church but I did not want to go in. I stayed in the car and kept it running. My father said, "Come on Elena, God is going to heal Abel tonight." It was a hillbilly revival. I stayed in the car for fifteen minutes; mom and dad were still inside. There were only three or four cars outside. I waited some more but then I thought I'd better go and see what is happening inside. I wanted to scold them, I was angry that they were taking the time to do this when we should be taking Abel to the hospital. I had no faith for healing like they did. I went inside the church thinking that

I would find them in the back pews but my parents were right in front of the Preacher and he was saying in a loud voice, "There is nothing impossible for God!" Abel was coughing so much; I could hear it all the way to the back and it was interrupting what the Preacher was saying. The Preacher finally said; "let's pray for this child so we can hear the message". He stepped down and gathered everybody around Abel and my parents and they started to pray out loud. He said, "We are going to pray until this child stops coughing so I can go back to my preaching." They started praying and kept praying. I think they prayed for thirty minutes while Abel just kept coughing like he never coughed before and I just kept watching them pray for my little brother. Then all of a sudden, Abel stopped coughing. He was silent and they all stopped praying and looked at Abel and my parents. My mother touched Abel and said his fever is gone and he is healed! Everyone started yelling, "He is healed". They were jumping for joy. One of them asked, "What was wrong with him?" When they found out that he had TB, they almost fell back, they were amazed. Mom took the microphone and started testifying about God's healing power and how her husband, my father, had both lungs with TB and God had healed him. The people were shocked and awed then the revival really started. Everyone began jumping and dancing in the Spirit. They were rejoicing and praising and giving glory to God. Abel never coughed again from that moment on and the revival went on full blast. I stood there in shock and amazement myself; seeing the healing power of God in my own family and right before my eyes.

After Abel received his healing, they started making plans to go back to San Antonio. My mother had something in her mind; she wanted to prove to the doctors that Abel was healed by God and totally free of TB. By this time, Abel was about three years old. They struggled with their decision because of the authorities in San Antonio that wanted to take Abel from them. The Health Department and the Police, who enforced the laws regarding TB patients, still had warrants and orders against them. They finally made up their mind and she was determined to show them the

Come Home, Son

power of God to heal. She wanted them to see that God healed my father and my brother, Abel.

I did not want to go with them. I wanted the best for them and wanted them to go but I wanted to stay in Chicago. I loved them very much but I did not want their Christian life. Everything worked for good; God had united us through all this suffering and God had prospered my father and the family. He always had a song and a smile on his face, people loved him, and he was truly transformed. Father always taught us about tithing so that we were always blessed. Mom always spoke faith, she said God does everything right. Mom knew more than the doctors, she knew her family would be healed and they were. My mind kept flashing back to that small country church we found that dark snowy night.

My father called San Antonio to see if he had a contract job to do. Harvest season was over in Chicago, it had already started snowing but I heard father say, "I'll take the truck to San Antonio." My father would shovel snow right alongside of his sons; he was feeling good and growing stronger every day. The doctors in Grand Rapids had said that he would not be able to drive for ten years and here it was only three months later and he was strong and able to do heavy work.

He headed back to San Antonio, driving a large 18-wheeler truck and took one of my brothers with him. When he got there he started transporting gravel. After just one week, he returned to Chicago to pick up his other truck and get his family. When he returned he told me that there was a lot of work in San Antonio and that he was going to Wisconsin to buy a new truck. So I went to Racine, Wisconsin with him to purchase a new truck. My father had his heart set on buying a red truck and the very first truck we saw was exactly what he wanted. He made the deal real quick and he got everything he wanted. He wanted me to come back with him but I told him that I needed to give my job notice because I did not want to burn any bridges in case I ever needed that job again. He kept on insisting and even offered to buy me my own truck and open up my own business but I told him I couldn't go yet. So they left and I stayed.

A couple of days later, he called me in Chicago and said that he had already found the exact truck he was going to purchase for me and that he had already given a down payment on it. It was a gorgeous black truck, just like I told him I would like. He said, as soon as you get here, we can go and get your truck. I got real excited about going back to San Antonio at that point and in a week; I was on my way home.

When I go there, we went right to the truck dealership and picked it up. My father was right, it was a beautiful truck and there was plenty of work in San Antonio. They were expanding the city, putting in new freeways and bridges and my father had a contract to transport gravel, sand and asphalt. We earned good money in those days so that I always had money and slowly I got back into drugs.

My mother prayed for me all the time. I later found out that her petition before the Lord was that I would not have a good time in the world. I had a lot of conviction on my life because of her prayers and I never enjoyed the partying, dancing, drinking at bars and such. I seldom wanted to be in public having a good time, as most people would do. I mostly kept to myself. I did not like the night life but I led a very different life from my parents.

In the back of my mind, I would remember the way I had been raised. I was raised a Christian and although I was not serving God at the time, I never enjoyed the good times of this world. I saw my friends having a good time in bars but I never could; I always felt uncomfortable in that environment. I would go in for a beer but I would not stay long because it was dangerous. I had become a drug dealer

CHAPTER FOUR

The Life of a Drug Dealer

DURING THOSE TEN YEARS, from 1959 through 1969, drugs were my life and my business. I had made up my mind not to use drugs, just make a business out of it and make plenty of money. I started buying and selling large amounts of drugs but you cannot play with fire and not get burned. I got burned! I got hooked. I became a junkie! I kept to myself as much as possible; I sold the drugs to dealers and pushers so that very few people knew my face. Many knew my name but few knew my face and that was the way I liked it. In the life of a drug dealer, there are killings, betrayals, junkies, peddlers and dealers always have many enemies. One day my father found a gun in my room and he said, "If you live by the sword, you will die by the sword. The one who lives with a gun will die by the gun." I wasn't saved but that scripture stayed with me for a long time. I would always remember it.

When I started in the drug business, I began by going to Mexico; I had connections in Nuevo Laredo. I could buy heroin real cheap there. I was all the way into drug dealing, yet I continued to see the hand of God in my life because He always took care of me. I was never knifed, beat up or jumped on. No bullets ever touched me.

Once I was crossing the International Bridge in Nuevo Laredo, getting to the other side was easy but it was not so easy coming back. I was with my connection from Mexico, a man named Chano, and he said to me, "Don't worry, I know how to get you across the border." We decided not to cross the bridge, Chano got us a lancha, which was the front fender of a model A car, we turned it upside down and used it as a boat to cross the Rio Grande River. Chano knew a man that would cross us over for $5.00; that way we did not have to cross the bridge because the American side had police watching out for us. This time two crossed over on the lancha, el Conejo was with me. We were caught by surprise as we were getting off. The American agents threw up flares and at the same time five policemen with rifles were yelling, "Federal Agents, Federal Agents!" The heroin was in my hands and when I heard them, I dove into the water and I yelled, "Jump in, Conejo, jump in. Tirate Hombre!" The water was only three feet deep but I dove into the water because there were bullets flying. I could see them flying past me. I wasn't afraid for my life; I just did not want to lose the heroin. Chano's wife, "La Huera" sold and prepared the heroin in waterproof bags, just in case it fell into the water; lucky for me. The flares stayed lit for a long time so I dove under the water to hide. The current took me to the left on the American side two or three blocks in the river. When I looked back, I did not see anyone so I hid by a tree floating in the river that was tangled on a branch, which ended up being my life saver. Bamboo sticks were all over and I had seen water moccasins in the river before. By now, it was after midnight, my heroin was still with me. I had taken some heroin earlier that day and was still high on it so I fell asleep on the trunk of that tree. I had decided to stay there all night but as soon as it was daylight, I went out to the bank of the river. I kept called; "Conejo! Conejo!" He never answered me. I never knew what happened to him but I figured he was dead.

I dug a hole in the sand and buried the drugs in it about six or seven in the morning. I walked down the road to the Cantina nearby but it was closed so I walked toward the bridge. I had left my car in Mexico and as I walked I thought about Chano and I had this horrible gut feeling that it was him. He was the one who had set us up! As I walked, I got angrier and angrier. I went across to the Mexican side to get my car. My clothes were dry by then. I went straight to Chano's house and I was very angry by the time I arrived. When Chano saw me, he eyes opened wide and I caught that look in his eyes. I knew that instant that I was right, it was him who set us up! Don Jose, the man from the lancha had probably told him that we were dead. Chano was a politician but he couldn't hide his surprise and guilt. Sure enough, it was him. Several men were there trying to score some drugs. There were American cars parked in front of his place; Lincolns, Cadillacs and Mercedes.

La Huera, Chano's wife, was at the scales and when she heard my voice, she ran out from the other room and put her arms around me. She was very happy to see me alive. She said, "We heard you were dead!" I said, "They didn't kill me but I'm pretty sure they killed Conejo!" I turned toward Chano, unable to talk because I was so mad. There was tense silence for a moment and then I said, "Chano, I believe you turned us in!" The other men that were there were listening intently. I continued, "What a coincidence that the Federal Agents just happened to be in the exact spot and the exact time we reach the American side. I am accusing you, Chano because I have a gut feeling and if I find out it is true, I am coming back to kill you and if I don't kill you, someone else will!" I caught a look in La Huera's face that led me to believe that she already knew. Huera and I had become friends and if she liked you, you got extra dope in your deal. She had liked me and Chano never knew. Chano was 70 years old and he had made a lot of money. Huera was only 35 years old.

Chano spoke, as he cocked a loaded gun and said, "If you are accusing me of setting you up or talk bad about me, I will kill you! In fact, Huera, I think I ought to kill him now!" Huera jumped in the middle of us and then she asked, "Where is the heroin?" I replied, "I lost it." She immediately said, "I will replace it, Sonny." Chano then put his gun away and went to go sit while he watched me. He kept his gun close to him. I didn't take the heroin from Huera, I just told her to give me enough for a fix. I knew I could not cross the bridge with heroin on me.

My car was at the Cantina so I went back and picked it up and drove home to San Antonio. I knew I had credit with La Huera so I sent someone else to get it and he was turned in by an informant and picked up at the bridge.

The Lord warned me so many times of danger. God watched out for me even in those bad days. I later found out Chano was working with the American Federal Agents who paid informants to point drug dealers out and U.S. Agents would give the heroin back to the connection and get a reward from them. So Chano got his heroin back and he just kept selling it. What a racket! He was double crossing his own customers and making money on both sides. He would make the sell and then he would get his product back. Chano was setting up only the ones he wanted, those he didn't particularly like for whatever reason. I don't know why he set me up. I was a regular customer but maybe he got jealous because his wife liked me.

Later in San Antonio, Conejo's mom came to my house looking for him. I told her, "I don't know where he is, he stayed in Laredo." She came by my house almost every week looking for him. She died never knowing that her son was killed that night we tried to cross the River. I never told her, I did not want her to get even more hurt. When I got home, my mother told me that she could not sleep all night and that she had dreamt water and bullets. She said, "I was afraid you were dead. What happened? Where were you, Sonny?" Every time something happened to me like that, mother seemed to know about it. After that incident my life was drugs and deals and always in danger.

I had to keep making trips to Mexico to run my drug business, even if Chano and I had threatened each other. La Huera found out where I was and started sending me shipments. We used a special code so that every time we talked no one would understand if someone was listening. Chano did not know about our deals and I have a feeling she kept money for herself. I went back to make a buy, his wife had sent me word with another addict, and warned me not to come. She said that I was very lucky that Chano had not killed me yet. She told me that Chano had threatened her and that if I came, he would kill her too.

Chano had a reputation of killing many men. His ranch was like a fortress. It was well known that at his ranch he had buried several men. Most of the men that worked for him ended up dead if they knew too much. Huera warned me not to take it lightly and not to come back. She said she would make sure I got my supply but I was never to go back to Chano's place again. I was tempted to go back many times because the arrangement I had with her was not working like I wanted since I had to pay someone else to pick up the shipment. In the drug business there are no friendships, just traitors. The man Huera chose to carry my shipments was Chango, who was a compadre. That didn't work out because he was a thief. There isn't a drug addict who is trustworthy.

Since I wasn't satisfied with that connection, we kept going to Laredo. I started looking for another connection. I started dealing with the Pineda Brothers from Nuevo Laredo, Mexico. I was still in danger because I had to cross over to Nuevo Laredo to buy from the traffickers and make arrangements to ship it to San Antonio. Sometimes, we made arrangements and traffickers kept the money and the drugs. I had to be careful who I did business with.

One day I was invited to a party in Laredo, Texas and was introduced to a young woman, ex-wife of a Customs Agent in Laredo. We started a conversation right away and she told me she had two little girls, ages nine and eleven, and that her husband had molested both her daughters. She was educated but confused about whether to press charges and bring it into the open. She did not want her daughters to grow up ashamed because of what happened to them. The drinks made it easy for her to talk to me. She and her husband were not living together and she told me that he would do anything to keep her from talking. She had him under control. He would buy her brand new cars but she would not have anything to do with him. He would try to keep her happy to keep her quiet. If the news that he had molested his daughters was found out, he would lose his job and he would go to prison. He was a "somebody" in Nuevo Laredo, he was on Federal payroll and had power and influence, more than a city cop. This woman wanted to leave Laredo and start all over again. She was in the process of making a deal with him where he would give her so much money every month and keep her in brand new cars. That was his hush money. They were making plans when she met me. Everyone at the party dealt in drugs so she knew I was in it too. She saw an opportunity to leave Laredo and asked if I could get her a house in San Antonio. She did not know her way around that city nor did she know anyone in San Antonio. She had money but she needed someone to help her get settled and she said, "If you help me, I will help you in your business." I told her I would help her. I did not think she knew anything about my business but apparently she knew more than I did. She followed me to San Antonio in her car. I had a brother in law I recommended to her to help her get a house and within a week, she was in a house.

The deal was that she would help me and she really wanted to get even with her husband so she knew that she could blackmail him into crossing the drugs. She had planned this all along but I did not know it. I had forgotten her part of the deal until she mentioned it. "Now, I am going to help you, Sonny. How do you bring the drugs across?" I said

I am not happy with the Pineda brothers because it is too dangerous. I am too involved in crossing over the drugs and I know that I can get caught or killed any time." She knew the Pineda brothers so her plan was to go buy the drugs and carry them across for me by having her husband help her. The drug connection knew she was the wife of a Customs Agent so they would not sell to her so I had to go with her to make the purchase. I made the purchase and loaded up the car. We went to a restaurant and she called her husband from there and talked him into meeting her. He agreed to pick her up because she told him that she wanted to be with him so he unknowingly helped cross the drugs and he never knew it. He may have found out about her

The Life of a Drug Dealer

later, I'm not sure. The one who carried the drugs was called a "mula", a mule. The mule carried the shipment or cargo of drugs.

After three years, she and I stopped doing business because she had become an addict and a dealer herself. She started getting greedy and well known and that made her very dangerous. I wanted to let her go. I had an uncle in Guadalajara who also had a drug lab so I contact him and he started sending me shipments on credit. He also sent shipments to Carrasco who eventually killed him. My uncle's shipments were cheaper and the heroin was pure.

When I started doing business with my uncle, my business exploded. We started to expand because I did not have to invest much money, hardly any because I did not have to pay for the product until I sold the drugs. If my uncle's shipments were confiscated, it was his loss, not me.

I met Lydia, my wife, when I was twenty-five years old. My father said to me one day, "Sonny, you need to settle down and get married so you can get out of this horrible life you are living. So I took his advice and got married. Lydia lived just next door to my parent's house. My parents rented a house to Lydia's family. So Lydia and I married but nothing changed. My life as a drug dealer only expanding. I was married to the drugs. Drugs were getting a stronghold in San Antonio and there were fights in the streets, new drug connections in Austin, Dallas, Fort Worth and Chicago. I was very ambitious and wanted to make a lot of money, I could not get enough. We started recruiting people to handle the demands of Austin, San Antonio, Dallas, Fort Worth and Houston. In those days, there weren't scanners or drug dogs so we shipped everywhere like UPS. The huge growth in drug dealing started a power struggle. Everyone wanted to control things. Carrasco was the first one to start. He wanted to control all the connections and control all the drug sales of San Antonio. We started moving north so we could control all of Dallas. We are the ones who controlled Dallas and later moved on to Houston. Carrasco had become very strong in drug dealing and was killing people. After a while, Dallas was the same, the dealers wanted to control the turf, it was about the barrios, territorial control.

There was a lot of greed with everyone fighting and killing each other for control of territories and money. The man who sold for me was named Chango and he was the one who distributed to all the dealers.

CHAPTER FIVE

The Kennedy Days

THE LAW BEFORE KENNEDY was abusive to the drug addict, President John F. Kennedy's inaugural address set a tone of youthful idealism that raised the nation's hopes. "Ask not what your country can do for you, ask what you can do for your country, he exhorted. Kennedy's wit and charm earned him considerable popularity at home and abroad. The government saw that drugs were going to destroy the United States. The politicians started having trouble with their own families, some of their children started using drugs. They saw the problem come right into their own homes. They knew they had to do something.

The Kennedy's opened a hospital in 1960, which was in Fort Worth, Texas, that focused on doing research to find the cause for drug addiction. They took volunteers and some like myself were court ordered. The government wanted guinea pigs so they could get inside their brain and find out the causes of drug addiction. Was it environmental, hereditary, child abuse or poverty? What caused it? With me, they never figured it out. I was not an abused child. I did not come from poverty. I had loving parents and they were good disciplinarians. I walked around feeling guilty with heaviness inside me all the time. I had no one to go to, no one cared for me. I was no good, everybody said I was no good; even pastors wouldn't talk to me. The condemned me and told me that I was going straight to the electric chair.

There were no laws to protect the drug addicts. The police used to abuse and beat them thinking that would force them off the drugs. Kennedy was to get involved in Civil Rights, including the civil rights of the drug addicts. Washington started to change the law and President Kennedy ordered federal troops to campus to suppress the resulting riots. To strengthen civil rights, President Kennedy sent to Congress a special message asking for legislation to desegregate public facilities and give the Justice Department authority to bring school integration suits. The drug addicts loved John F. Kennedy because he was a sort of "deliverer" to them. Some time ago, the "whites" used to beat up the blacks and the Mexicans. When Martin Luther King came alone, he preached education and equal right, he was the "deliverer" to the Blacks. Before Dr. King, the Blacks didn't know they had rights, they couldn't vote and there was segregation and inequality, especially in the South. Martin Luther King set them free, he had a dream, he was the son of a Pastor and he completed his mission.

President Kennedy did the same for the drug addict. The addict could not vote; they did not have a voice. They were not allowed a driver's license. The police would plant drugs on them to send them to prison. The law would also arrest your family and the sentences were heavy. When Kennedy came along, there were grants, civil rights and prisoner's right in the penitentiary. President Kennedy got involved in the prison system and started using federal guard in the prison to keep oversight of the prison system. He brought prison reform. Civil rights brought new changes and new laws so that the drug addict looked up to Kennedy where previously they had been treated like dogs. Now President Kennedy gave them freedoms, the government started to see drug abuse as an illness.

The Narcos (narcotic agents) used to tell us the government was going to put us in space ships and throw us into outer space. They also would put us in mental hospitals and give us shock treatments, I wouldn't take them. I would fight the nurses and started yelling and fighting. I would call my attorney, Anthony Nicholas and Roy Barrera, Sr. I always had their business card handy and would call them right away.

First, they gave us a drug named Torazin, this drug causes you to lose control of your body functions. You don't know who you are; they wanted to play with your mind while you were under this drug. Sometimes the narcos would take you to some kind of kangaroo count. To an office with a man with a big hat and he would send you for six (6) months to South Presa, the crazy house in San Antonio, it was the State Mental Hospital. There was no justice. The narcos would throw you in that room and say, "I got another dope fiend, Judge." How could they sentence you without a lawyer? Then when you got to the hospital, you would get the shock treatments for months; by that time that person went out of his mind.

I know someone named Hope Lozano who has been there since the 1950's and she is still there. When you got there, you really had to make a racket. I escaped from that State Mental Hospital many times, first chance I would get. I would take the bus downtown, but this time, I was in my twenties. Many addicts from those years may still be in that hospital. The treatments were not to help you kick the habit but to make you insane to keep you in there. Mike Linares went through those shock treatments and he was never right in his mind after that. One time he went in and never came out. I heard later that another patient slit Mike's throat. Fred Perez, a member of this Church was a patient in the State Mental Hospital also when he was a drug addict. He is now 64 years old and he has never been the same since he received those shock and drug treatments. The shock treatments slow you down and make you retarded.

The government had a Japanese encampment in Fort Worth that they had taken over and converted into a drug rehabilitation center. There were still some Japanese left behind because of mental illness. Even though the war was over, some Japanese were treated like prisoners.

The big drug push was on; I was in it up to my neck. By 1960,

I had a successful transport business. I owned several trucks and used them to transport drugs. Finally, one day in Dallas, it all came down. They caught up with me and several other business associates, restaurant owners and gas station owners. We were all involved in a large chain of drug trafficking.

On November 22 at 12:30pm, while riding in an open limousine through Dallas, Texas, President Kennedy was shot in the head and neck by a sniper bullet. He was rushed to Parkland Memorial Hospital where efforts to save him failed. President John Fitzgerald Kennedy died that day. The state funeral for President Kennedy's assassination was watched on television by millions all around the world. I was charged and had court that same week. My trial Judge was Sarah Hughes, who was the same Federal Judge who swore in Lyndon B. Johnson for President of the United States of America just after Kennedy's death was announced to the world. The entire gang of traffickers was being tried that same week. They were all chained together in front of Judge Hughes as she handed down very stiff sentences giving everyone fifty years in prison.

Judge Sarah Hughes took me to the front and asked me if I had something to say. I said, "No". Lydia, my wife, was there with our first born son, Jesse. The lawyer was pleading for me and telling Judge Hughes that this was our first child and that he was only two months old and that I was just twenty-five years old. Lydia came forward that day in court and the Judge kept looking at baby Jesse and I and she said, "I see something in you, Mr. Perales." She had already sentenced everyone else in this trafficking ring to fifty years in Levenworth Federal Prison. She said, "If I sentenced you to fifty years, I will be sending your son to prison too." She was right, I thought to myself. She then said, "I am going to sentence you to fifty years in Levenworth like the others but I am going to review your case before you leave for Levenworth. I want to see you again before you leave."

The Federal Agent prosecuting my case got very upset and said, "We have been looking for this man for many years, and he always escapes. Your Honor, we have provided pictures and evidence that shows we have caught him red-handed. Why are you giving him special consideration? He has been indicted twice for murder and twice he has been let go."

Everyone else was left in chains and taken back to County jail but Judge Hughes wanted me to stay behind because she wanted to talk to me some more. She took a break and I was left un-cuffed outside the courtroom in the hallway. There were a couple of Federal Agents standing by but I could have escaped, if I really wanted to, even my attorney could not understand it. When the Judge came back, she asked if I had ever had probation. With my type of case, one is usually not given probation. She started talking about the Kennedy program which was called Nara. Nara 1, Nara 2 and Nara 3, which represented the three different stages of the program.

Most of the drug traffickers had been business men, in it for the money and greed. I had been in it for the money too but I was also a user, a drug addict addicted to heroin. Judge Hughes offered me that program. She asked me if I would like to be a guinea pig for five years instead of fifty years in prison. She explained that Nara was a program for psychiatric research and that after five years I would be released. She also mentioned a new drug called Methadone. The Federal government, at that time, did not know the addictive and dangerous effects of Methadone. They did not know that it was just a substitute for heroin and just as addictive.

They wanted to experiment with us to find out why we used drugs. I was only in Nara for a short while and then I was sent to welding school. I was one of the very first groups in the Nara Program. The first groups of guinea pigs were very scared, they had heard wild stories about methadone and one of those stories was that it could cause cancer and that it could kill you, which is true. When we arrived, they had an orangutan, bigger than a man, a huge monkey, which they experimented with by getting him hooked on drugs. The doctors would give us a tour and take us to see this monkey. They had trained the monkey so that when he had the urge for a fix, he would pull a cord and the light bulb would light up and the doctor would come and the monkey would get his arm out ready for the fix. The monkey was purposely hooked on drugs by the doctors so that they could study the drug addiction habit. He started requiring an injection three to four times a day. Until one day, the doctors would not give him anymore and the monkey got very sick while breaking the habit. The monkey broke the habit and was healed and then they tried another experiment by letting the guard turn on the light bulb which meant that the doctor would come in with a fix for the monkey. The orangutan would go berserk when he would see the light come on. He would run to the opposite corner of his cage when he saw the doctor entering with the needle. The monkey would get very angry; he did not want to get hooked again. The doctors used that as an example and they would say, "See even the monkey knows better than to go back on the drug." Was the monkey smarter than man?

Drug dependence, psychological and sometimes even the physical state are characterized by a compulsion to take a drug in order to experience its psychological effects. Addiction is a severe form of dependence, usually marked by physical dependence. The latter state exists when the drug has produced physiological changes in the body as evidenced by the development of tolerance (increasing amounts of the drug are needed to achieve the same effect) and of a withdrawal syndrome after the drug's effects have worn off. The syndrome is marked by symptoms such as nausea, diarrhea, pain and these vary with the type of drug used. Psychological dependence, or habituation, is present when the compulsion to take a drug is strong, even in the absence of physical withdrawal symptoms.

Scientists often measure a drug's potential for abuse by studies with laboratory animals. Drugs that an animal will administer to itself repeatedly are said to have powerful reinforcing properties and a high potential for abuse. Examples include some of the major abused drugs such as opium, alcohol, cocaine and barbiturates. Other drugs, such as marijuana and other hallucinogens appear to produce habituation in humans even though they are not powerful re-enforcers for laboratory animals. Commonly abused drugs, besides substances such as alcohol and tobacco, can be grouped into six classes. Those classes are; opioids, sedative-hypnotics, stimulants, hallucinogens, cannabis and inhalants.

Opioids

This class includes drugs derived from opium, such as morphine and heroin and its synthetic substitutes such as methadone. Medically, morphine is a potent pain reliever; it is the standard by which other pain-relieving drugs are measured. It and other opium derivatives also suppress coughing, reduce movements of the intestine, providing relief from diarrhea and induce a state of psychological indifference. Heroin, a preparation synthesized from morphine, was introduced in 1898 as a cough suppressant and non-addicting substitute for morphine. The addictive potential of heroin was soon recognized and its use was prohibited in the United State, even in medical practice.

Users report that heroin produces a "rush" or a "high" immediately after it is taken. It also produces a state of profound indifference and may increase energy.

The drug produces different effects under different circumstances. The drug taker's past experience and expectations have some influence, as does the method of administering the drug, whether it is by injection, ingestion or inhalation. Symptoms of withdrawal include kicking movements in the legs, anxiety, insomnia, nausea, sweating, cramps, vomiting, diarrhea and fever.

Early American Prisons

In America, the concept of imprisonment came to realization. Spurred by deep religious beliefs, the English Quaker William Penn, founder of the colonies of Pennsylvania, abolished the death penalty for most crimes in the late 1600s, substituting imprisonment instead as punishment. The colonists, however, were compelled by the British government in 1718 to reinstate the death penalty. In 1789, shortly after independence, the Pennsylvania legislature replaced capital punishment with incarceration as the primary punishment for felons. The Walnut Street Goal (Jail), in Philadelphia, became the first prison in the United States of America. By the mid-19th century, most States had followed suit.

Two models soon emerged in the States. The first system began in Auburn State Prison in New York in 1817. Prisoners worked together in total silence during the day but were housed separately at night. Strict discipline was enforced and violators were subjected to severe reprisals. The second model, the Pennsylvania system, which began in 1829 in the Eastern State Penitentiary at Cherry Hill, was based on solitary confinement for convicts by day and night.

Vigorous debate erupted between proponents of the two systems. Those favoring the Pennsylvania model focused on its hope of rehabilitation, the theory being that a felon, alone in a cell with only the Bible to read, would soon become penitent (hence the term penitentiary). The Auburn system was criticized as being virtual slavery because prisoners there were often put to work for private entrepreneurs who had contracted with the State for their labor. Furthermore, prisoners were never paid, thus leaving handsome profits for the business owners and the State. Advocates of the Auburn system, however, alleged that the idleness of the prisoners in the Cherry Hill penitentiary sometimes caused madness. Proponents of the Auburn system stressed the activity of the prisoners and the profits from their labor, which meant the State did not have to finance the prison.

Most States found the argument based on profit irresistible and adopted the Auburn approach. European countries, however, emulated the Pennsylvania model, primarily as a result of a report by the French writer, Alexis de Tocqueville, who went to the United State to investigate the two systems so as to inform the French government of their respective merits.

The Goal of Rehabilitation

The primary objective of both the Auburn and Pennsylvania systems was the confinement of prisoners for the duration of their sentences. Thus, the facilities themselves were usually massive institutions, with high stone walls, substantial perimeter security and restriction of prisoner movement. Some of those prisons are still in use today. By the mid-19th century, however, penologists began to argue that prisoners could and should be rehabilitated while incarcerated.

In 1870, the National Congress on Penitentiary and Reformatory Discipline, now known as the American Correctional Association, met for the first time in Cincinnati, Ohio. The Congress adopted a set of principles for corrections, chief of which was the primacy of the goal of rehabilitation. This led to the establishment for juvenile offenders of so-called reformatories, championed by the American penologist, E. C. Wines and Zebulon Brockway. Although their attempts to rehabilitate were relatively unsuccessful, the goal of rehabilitation changed the criminal justice system in the following decades. Probation and parole, work release, community corrections and even a separate system of procedures and courts for dealing with juvenile offenders can all be traced back to the ideals first enunciated in 1870.

Restrictions on Prison Labor

Concomitantly, the industrial prison of the Auburn model was coming under increasingly severe attacks. It had always been opposed by private business, which considered the unpaid prison labor unfair competition. Early trade unions in the North also challenged the idea but with little effect. As labor influence grew in the late 19th and early 20th centuries, however, dramatic changes occurred. By the 1920s, labor critics, joined by the humanitarian critics, achieved their aim of severely restricting prison labor. The U.S. Congress enacted the Hawes-Cooper Act in 1929 which divested prison-made goods of the protection afforded by the Interstate Commerce Act and made such goods subject to State punitive laws. During the depression of the 1930s, Congress completed the task by prohibiting transport companies from accepting prison-made products for transportation into any State in violation of the laws of that State. This legislation, the Ashurst-Sumners Act of 1935, effectively closed the market to goods made by prisoners and most States then terminated prison industry.

Changes in the Prison System

Confronted with thousands of prisoners who would otherwise be idle, American prison systems rapidly re-embraced the idea of rehabilitation as the principal goal of incarceration. Social scientists, moreover, sought to provide methods by which prisoners could be classified according to their likelihood of rehabilitation so that their specific needs could be articulated. The fortress like prison was recognized as being unsuitable for prisoners who could truly be reformed and a wide variety of institutions, including reformatories, work camps and minimum-security prisons were established. By the 1960s, this general trend was augmented by the concept of community corrections, in which prisoners would work in the communities by day but return to an institution at night. Work release centers, community correctional centers and halfway houses, all with minimal security, were established.

Rehabilitation Programs

Programs such as vocational training, guidance counseling and psychotherapy were begun within the prison system to achieve the major goal of rehabilitation. In 1975, however, a study of more than 240 such programs essentially concluded that none was truly successful in reducing the recidivism rate (the rate of repeat offenders). Although this study was immediately criticized by some, many penologists have agreed with its basic conclusions. Participation in these programs was often more motivated by the hope that the parole board would look favorably on those prisoners who enrolled. Most penologists also now agree that rehabilitation is not a proper reason for imprisoning someone. Concomitant with these changing views, a movement was begun to preclude parole boards from knowing whether or not a prisoner had participated in such a program. Thus, rehabilitation is no longer the only, or even the main, objective of the corrections agencies.

Prison Population and Housing

In theory, the U.S. Prison System today consists of a variety of institutions, each adapted to the characteristics and risks posed by its population. In fact, however, that is not the case. A recent survey showed that more than 50 percent of all prisoners continued to be housed in maximum-security facilities, even though penologists agree that no more than 15 percent of the population requires such secure housing. Similarly, only 11 percent of the prison population is housed in minimum-security institutions, even though correctional systems personnel are virtually unanimous in their belief that at least one-third of all prisoners could safely be housed in such facilities. Pronounced differences exist between these two kinds of prisons.

Maximum-security institutions are massive buildings with high masonry walls or electrified fences in which the primary concern is security. Prisoners are under constant surveillance, their movements are severely restricted and many are required to remain in their cells almost the entire day. Outdoor recreation is minimal and visits, when allowed, are often conducted by telephone with a glass partition between the prison and the visitor.

Minimum-security prisons, on the other hand, are often built on a campus-like arrangement, which allows prisoners autonomy and freedom within broad bounds. Prisoners may have rooms with opaque doors rather than cells that are under constant surveillance. Visits are usually private and rarely monitored, close contact with visitors is encouraged in order to enhance the prisoner's ties with family and community. Some prisons have even experimented with conjugal visitations, allowing the prisoner to spend up to 72 hours with a spouse or other family members in separate housing such as a trailer. Such visitation programs are common in the Scandinavian countries.

In the U.S., a major impediment to modernizing the prison housing system is the burgeoning American prison population. In 1945 approximately 133,000 persons were confined in State and Federal prisons and reformatories. This figure rose slowly to about 180,000 in 1971. In the following years, the prison population escalated sharply to more than 500,000 by mid-1986. In view of these increases, prison personnel have been concerned with the immediate problems of overcrowding and the tensions this causes, rather than with the long-range issues of establishing a new housing pattern for convicted criminals.

Prison Organization

All American prison systems today are highly centralized, in contrast to the situation in the last century; where each prison was managed as a separate institution; without regard to other facilities in the same State. This centralization has generally led to increased professionalism among wardens and other prison staff. In earlier days, wardens were selected on the basis of political favoritism, often without any qualifications, training or experience in corrections. The jails that are used to hold persons pending trial or those serving sentences of less than one year, are typically not part of the State prison system. They are managed individually by the districts or counties in which they are located. Only a few States have an integrated prison and jail system, which allows for much greater flexibility in placing short-term prisoners in locations near their homes. Most local jail systems still reflect the same kind of political patronage that until recently characterized the prison system. The County Sheriff or other person assigned to manage the jail often has little experience in or any concern about corrections. This system has been severely criticized by many penologists, who have stated that the jails are the worst part of the U.S. penal organization.

CHAPTER SIX

A Vision in Hell

A DAY THAT LIVED with me for a long time was when Chango and his wife came to my house. They were very excited. He said, he was running because one of our peddlers wanted to kill him. He wanted some advice and asked me, "Sonny, should I kill him?" I told him exactly what to do. Look Chango, when he comes in to report the money, they get a new bag, right? Give him an overdose. The guy is strung out. Remember that he is using. The batch you usually give him has been cut four or five times, his body is used to that. What you need to do is give him pure heroin that hasn't been cut at all. That way he will overdose. When he arrives take out the pure heroin, he won't know the difference. Put it out on the table. Since it is free, he is going to take more. He'll think it is the one that is cut and will take more of the pure heroin than normal and he will overdose. You will put out two outfits, (a syringe fix) one for him and one for her; that way both will overdose. Chango left and I had helped him to plan two murders.

Later that night, Chango called me and said, "Sonny, they are both dead! But the problem is that they are both in my living room." I ran over there; it was about midnight. I made sure they were both dead. We took them by their feet and dragged them out near the garbage cans. I told Chango to go to sleep and if anyone asked, you didn't hear anything. No one ever found out. Everyone figured that they died of an overdose. This was my downfall. Things were never the same for me after that, I felt guilty all the time.

The next day I left for Dallas and drove to San Antonio to collect some money. I had called my peddler before I left Dallas. When I drove to his house, I was heading west on Castroville Road towards General McMullen Road. All of a sudden I heard noise coming from the trunk of my car. I heard someone kicking around in my trunk. I pulled into Las Palmas Shopping Mall to check it out. I got off and went to the truck to open it. There was no one there. I got back in the car and this time I heard someone laughing in the back seat. I couldn't imagine what it was but from that day on I started hearing noises and voices.

I started living in hell. I started living in fear for the next three years. There were nights that I could not sleep. I started seeing things. I could see the wind. Normally people can't see wind but I could. I saw bugs in the air, millions of them taking form. They formed into a face and then slowly formed into a complete human body. What is going on? I didn't know what to do. I started living a nightmare. A demon visited me at night and went into my closet. I had a German shepherd dog that could sense the demon before I did. The dog knew the demon was in the closet. Even though I lived in horror, I did not think I was going insane but my wife, Lydia, sure did. Although she never saw the things I saw, she knew something was terribly wrong. She was never molested by those demons; they did not bother her at all, just me. Sometimes I saw a green demon sitting right next to me, his face was making fun of me but Lydia never saw it. Fear paralyzed me. Lydia asked me, "Sonny, what is wrong?" I never knew such fear. I would break out in cold sweats and have to change into fresh clothes. It was pure fear. I had never experienced fear before. Lydia asked, "Sonny are you going crazy?" I didn't know how to make it stop.

One night during Christmas, Lydia invited me to church. The church was about two blocks from our house. During the

A Vision in Hell

service my mind kept thinking, "I don't want to be like these Holy Rollers, but I need help." Maybe if I go just for a little while, all this will go away and I'll be okay. I was hallucinating by this time and I didn't use hallucinating drugs. What am I going to do? When we got home from church that night, Lydia started to really talk to me. She said, "Sonny, if you give yourself completely to God, we could have a different life. Jesus loves you. He will protect you." I started thinking about those words. I meditated on them. Maybe this time Lydia was right. I had to do something.

All of a sudden I started seeing the wind again. I got up and hugged Lydia out of fear. I said, "Lydia, there it is again, let's go to bed. The thing started to take form again, I knew this time it was different. This time they were bigger. They were mosquitoes; millions and millions of gnats forming a figure only this time much bigger. The last one always made fun of me. I was paralyzed with fear because I knew things were getting worse. I knew from the moment it started formed at the Christmas tree. The face of this one was mad. He was communicating with my mind. The demon's teeth were like fangs with saliva coming out of his mouth. I knew he was going to attack me. He spoke to my mind. I call out, "Lydia, this one is going to attack me!" I grabbed her and put her on top of me. Lydia stated to pray rebuking the demons. The demon left. I realized that Lydia's words had power. God was starting to get my attention and was teaching me about His power. It seemed like a very long night but I finally went to sleep.

One night, as I was about to eat tamales, I saw the demons again. I just could not eat. I was getting desperate. I decided to go to church. It was raining and I was driving my brand new 1968 Mustang. I stopped right in front of my younger brother, Joel, who thought I was in Dallas at this time. We went inside the church and after the service my brother asked me for a ride to La Puente, California. He needed a ride to get to the Bible School he was going to attend but I told him that I could not take him. I decided to go straight home. That night I saw that demon again. He paralyzed me with fear for several hours. What could I do?

It was about three or four in the morning when my cousin,

Mike, called. He was upset. He said, "There are a lot of police raids going on because pushers are selling to an informant. You and I sold to him, Sonny. Mike was very agitated and continued, "They are picking up people left and right." Mike told me he was going to Chicago for a while because things were too hot in San Antonio.

An informant works for the police by introducing a rookie cop trained in drug dealing. This cop is usually brought in from out of town so that he is not recognized. He gathers information on the deals going down and the buys he sets up. He takes the name of the dealer, address and the amount of drugs they bought. Informants give the information to the narcs and this information becomes evidence. When this evidence is prepared by the narc, it is given to the District Attorney. The DA then refers to this as the indictment. These are called sealed indictments. The reason they are sealed is so that no one finds out who the informant is until they have built up cases on at least 100 or more. Then they round up the offenders as soon as possible because after the round up the word gets out and they will find out who the informant is and that informant cannot be used anymore. The informant is then given witness protection or sent to another town to start doing the same thing. An informant is usually a drug addict himself who has a case against him and has worked out a deal for a reduced sentence. In many case, his life span is very short, he ends up getting killed or commits suicide. I knew I had to get out too. Then I remembered my brother Joel. He wants to go to California so I call him. I told him that I would take him to the Bible School in La Puente, California.

As I saw it, my problem was not with God. I knew He was there all the time. I knew there was a God and that He took care of me. I would pray to God at night asking Him not to leave me behind. It was my own fault that I did not want to get saved or obey. I knew that even thought I was a sinner, God heard my prayers.

Demons can control your mind when you leave a door open which can happen to people who use drugs like I did or rebel

A Vision in Hell

against God like I did by refusing to become a Christian. I rejected Jesus over and over again. When you reject the gospel, you give the devil dominion over you. I believe people can be hindrances to their own salvation like with Bartamaeus. The way a Christian hinders others by their testimony or lifestyle. The way Christians live are examples, holy in church yet out of church they live like hell. They beat their wives and in church they call themselves deacons. Some also had lovers outside of their marriage. This was a huge hindrance to me. I said to myself I better stay a drug addict. Harassed by demons caused me to get mad at God. My friends did not believe me. Pastors would not listen to me unless I was a thither. My thought was, "How can I give my ten percent if I am not even saved?" Worse, I was tormented by demons.

The demons stayed about two hours this time; just enough to bother me. I ran outside the house to the back yard and I started talking to God like a mad man. I was going crazy by this time. I said, "God, why don't you just take me? You are the giver of life, just take my life. Why did you bring me into this world anyway? I know that you are the one that created me, you made me. I prefer living in hell. I don't want to continue living like this, send me to hell?" I just kept screaming to God. "I know you are real; I know you exist. I know you are punishing me but when is it going to stop?" I was tired of being tormented by the demons. I had been going through this horrible nightmare for three years and toward the end of the last year, I was just so tired of the battle. No one knew the battle I was going through. They wouldn't have believed me. They would have thought I was crazy. Lydia knew something was going on because every time the demons visited me, my bed was all wet with sweat.

I was able to function in the daytime in the business sense. I liked business and had a head for business. But in the evening, I was another person. After the demons came, I was left completely drained, totally exhausted. I had to get up and put on clean clothes. My high had left so I had to get another fix. I was so tired of my life and I wanted out. "God, stop the world, I want off!"

The religious people would not believe me for sure. They did not love me. One day Lydia asked me to go and talk to the Pastor. I went and the Pastor told me I was in that condition because I didn't tithe. Tithe, I thought to myself, how could I tithe, I wasn't even saved. Tithing to that Pastor was more important than helping me. Forget about salvation and deliverance! Jesus came to save that which was lost. He only comes to the sick not to the healthy.

Luke 5:31: Jesus answered them, "It is not the healthy who need a doctor, but the sick. I have not come to call the righteous but sinners to repentance."

I had reached a point where I did not know what to think or what to do. My mind was messed up. I wanted God to tell me how long He was going to punish me. The death of those two people kept haunting me. I kept thinking about them and that day at Chango's house when we dragged their dead bodies out to the garbage cans. The guilt was driving me insane. The scripture kept coming to my mind that in heaven there will be no murderers so I felt that I had no hope. I knew some Scripture but I didn't know how to apply it. By this time, I had gotten so confused.

"God, if you are going to send me to hell anyway, do it now. I really believed the scripture."

Revelation 21:8 "But the cowardly, the unbelieving, the vile, the murderers, the sexually immoral, those who practice magic arts, the idolaters and all liars, their place will be in the fiery lake of burning sulfur. This is the second death."

I was a murderer and I believed that all murderers would go straight to hell. I screamed at the top of my lungs like a madman. "God, I am suffering anyway, do it now, send me now, send me to hell, why wait any longer. I really didn't know what I was saying. I was talking out of my head. And yet at this time I was going through another struggle inside of me. No one knew because I didn't dare tell anyone but in the inner most of my being I heard another small voice and it was telling me that I was going to preach someday. I saw myself preaching at Sinai Church. I was so confused. What is this? How can I be hearing that I am going to preach and going to hell too? I was afraid and so desperate.

It was about this time that I gave myself an over dose. We

A Vision in Hell

had been short on drugs. We had been waiting for a new shipment but it was confiscated at the border. I had to send men to go out and make a buy. When they arrived with the shipment, I took the first fix. They were my drugs so I went first but I took too much and accidently gave myself an overdosed. Pete and Chango thought I was dead. They put my body on a bed in one of the rooms. The house we were in was a drug connection house so that addicts came in all day long to buy drugs and to get their fix. The room was in full view of everyone coming and going. When the addicts came to buy, they could see me lying on the bed. They thought nothing of it. They thought it was just another addict on a high and sleeping it off but my guys knew that I had accidently overdosed.

It was during this time that I had a vision or a dream, I am not sure, all I know is that I saw myself on top of a mountain of sand. The mountain kept slipping away from under my feet. I could see down the valley and what appeared to be very small people. The mountain was breaking apart under me. As I was slipping down the valley, I heard the most horrible sounds I had ever heard. The closer I got, I realized the sounds were coming from those people. As I was falling, I saw a four leaf clover and I hung on to it. The clover had a long thin root that looked like a fine thread which did not break. I saw ugly gray smoke. I realized I was on my way to hell! I couldn't make out the sounds, whether they were made by men or women. They knew my name, though and they yelled in a high pitched desperate voice and said, "Sonny, don't come here, go back, Sonny, you do not want to come here, go back, Sonny, go back!"

I had heard sounds of torment like those of a woman whose husband got killed or whose child died but these screams were different; you couldn't make out the sounds. Was it a man or a woman? Their voices were all high pitched with pain and torment. It sounded like people who were burning. I didn't see any flames, only smoke. Everything looked ugly and grey. The people who called my name seem to know me but I did not know them. I was terrified. I knew this was not where I wanted to go. How could I have asked God to send me there? All of a sudden I remembered my mother's scripture. Psalm 46:1 "God is our refuge and strength, a very present help in trouble. Therefore, we will not fear, though the earth be removed and though the mountains be carried into the midst of the sea."

I repented because I knew where I was. I had been trying to get away from the demon and here he was. "Oh, God, I don't want to be in hell." I was hanging on to that thin thread or root but the demons were pulling my feet. I saw a thin line like a falling star. It was a light. I fell into something like a bowl of light. Inside the bowl of light was a cross and I had fallen into it. I did not see anyone standing there. Everyone fell back. They looked dead. As far as I could see, it looked like a swamp, a grayish green color. It looked foggy but it wasn't fog. It was a mist of smoke and a horrible smell like sulfur. The people looked like dwarfs. The one who had been tormenting me was there. I started yelling to God asking Him to save me and get me out of there. I prayed that scripture from Psalm "God is my refuge...Oh, God! Please forgive me and get me out of here!"

In the meantime, Pete and Chango had to wait till it got dark so they could take me out. They thought that I was dead so they put my body in the trunk. They threw me in so hard that I hit a piece of tire wrench and I woke up. First thing I did was look for my money and wallet, which, of course, Pete had already taken. He said, "Here, Sonny, I was holding it for you." Sure he was, I thought to myself. They were scared. I was alive and Chango had taken my watch and my rings. They had already sold all my drugs. Sure they were glad to see me, I bet.

After the vision, you would think I would straighten out but no; I went back to drugs even though I knew it was not a dream. I was convinced I had actually gone to hell. Afterwards, the demon kept coming back to me. I believe that the demon's mission was assigned to make me kill myself or drive me insane. God gives you the desires of your heart, even to sinners, so He showed me hell since I was asking for it. But, when I asked for forgiveness, God showed me His mercy. I saw a light, a white light. I still see it

A Vision in Hell

once in a while. God showed me His power even in hell. Everyone in hell was slain with the power of His light. After the vision, I never asked God to send me to hell.

The last time I saw that demon was Christmas of 1969. I saw him in the Christmas tree. After that Joel and I went to California. My brother, Joel never knew that I was running from San Antonio because the police were coming down hard on my drug business. The police were looking for me; they had already rounded up 102 addicts and dealers. The informant was a friend of mine who worked for me and I sold drugs to him. I did not know the "perros" (dogs) had a case on him. The perros had enough on me, of all the 102 addicts and dealers, all went to prison except Mike and I. We never found out if they ever made a case on us. I do not know if it was God or Mike's warning because if I had been caught I would still be in jail to this day.

I went to gather all my drugs to take them with me to California. I had a big habit and I wanted to make sure I had enough for my drug needs. I put the powder in a big long balloon. I had received the dope from the guys in grams so I couldn't bring it in the car. So I thought about using a balloon to hide them. I inserted the powder into a balloon and it got fat, about three inches round. I put the syringe inside the same balloon tied it with a knot and hid it in the car. The '68 Mustang had the gas tank in the center of the bumper right on top behind the license plate. I put the balloon there. The gas tank had a funnel. The balloon fit inside that funnel. I put a little string attached to the balloon that held it in place. When I put the gas cap on, the string would hold the balloon in place. I was desperately hooked. Joel picked up a friend named Mary Lou from his church that was also going to Bible School. They went to sleep right away in the car. It was about 3am when we finally got on the road.

On the way to California, it seemed that we stopped every two hours because I would have to get a fix. I had reached a point where I no longer got the feeling of the high. I know it was God taking the high out of the fix. The heroin seemed to have lost its effect on me, it had no strength and although I was taking more than I should, I did not get sick. I had been driving that night when I had another experience. I saw an elephant as big as a house. It was completely dark, in the middle of the night, so I had on the bright lights and I saw the elephant. I tried to wake up Joel. The elephant was in front of my lights and even though I was going sixty miles an hour, the elephant crossed in front of my car. I slammed on the brakes. Joel and Mary Lou fell off their seats. Joel got scared. He thought I had hit something. I said, "The elephant crossed in front of us." He thought I was joking but I was completely serious. "Look, Joel, don't you see it? It is right there!" The car was almost under the elephant's belly. The elephant must have been going to California too. I began driving slowly. The elephant's trunk covered the entire road. Joel and May Lou woke up; they thought I was playing around with them but I was dead serious. We were on Highway 90 going toward Uvalde, Texas so I stopped the car. I did not get out but I kept telling them that there was an elephant on the road. Joel said, "I don't see an elephant." Mary Lou was laughing out loud, she was sure I was just joking with them. I wasn't playing at all; I really did see an elephant in front of us. Joel asked, "What is the elephant doing?" I said, "He is looking at me. His trunk is wagging". It felt like the trunk was literally hitting the bumper of my car. Joel said, "Let's go, Sonny, we have to go." I said, "The elephant is right there, I can't go." They laughed even more. They never knew I was on drugs. But I knew it wasn't because of the heroin because heroin does not cause hallucinations. I drove all night and saw the elephant the whole time. No one else saw it. Every so often I stopped to inject myself with more drugs. When I got to the gas station, the elephant would be there alongside me. He never harmed us. In the morning, the elephant disappeared when Joel drove. When I drove at night, I would see the elephant again. When I got to California, I never saw the elephant again. I believe now it was a spiritual battle. The elephant represented the demons. They were letting me know they were still around.

CHAPTER SEVEN

Set Free and Called

> "But you are a chosen generation, a royal priesthood, a holy nation, His own special people, that you may proclaim the praises of Him **who called you out of darkness into His marvelous light."** 1Peter 2:9

I HAD A LOT OF HEROIN with me when we got to California. We went straight to the Bible School campus. The school was on Christmas vacation so there was no one in the dormitories. We stayed in the men's dorm and Mary Lou stayed in the women's dorm. My plans were to leave Joel in La Puente and move on. I had to go on to Tijuana, Mexico to make connection so I could get more drugs. I knew people in TJ. Since the heroin seemed to have lost its effect on me, I was using more and more. I believe it was God working in me, even then. Something supernatural was happening because I was not feeling the effects of that powerful drug anymore. No matter how much I took, I was not getting the level of high that I wanted, I just couldn't get there. I have seen God removed the desire for drugs in an instant from addicts who have been under the influence for many years. I have seen this kind of healing in the ministry.

We were in the dorm and I put the heroin in my pocket. I knew no one there would take it away from me. They didn't know I had it. In the morning, we went to get some coffee. I went to a garage to make a fix for me. I had plans but God had His own plans for me. I kept going to the bathroom taking as many fixes as I could, trying to get that high but nothing was happening. By Sunday, I was almost out of heroin. I thought to myself, "I can't run out". I had been waiting too long to get to Tijuana to buy more drugs and now Joel and some of his friends had taken my car without my permission. One of his friends had a relative who was a Pastor of a church nearby and they had taken the car, that Sunday, to go minister at that church. Joel plays the piano and sings so I guess that is what they were doing. Here I had planned to take off that day but now I did not have my car. By Monday night I was starting to get real sick and on Tuesday the bible school classes would resume. I said, "Joel, I am going to get sick, I have been using drugs all this time and now I've run out, I have to leave this morning before I get really sick." Joel asked me to meet his friends first. I really did not want to meet anybody; can't Joel see that I am sick?

I finally agreed to meet his friends so we had to go to the bible class where they were that day. The class had already started when we got there. The teacher's name was Rena. I sat in the back. The presence of God was filling that room. I had never felt that before, Rena had spiritual gifts. I did not know what they were but I started feeling extremely agitated and uncomfortable. Rena said, "Let's pray, I sense God wants to speak to us." That sister brought a message in tongues and the message was, "Don't hardened your heart, I brought you here. I want to save you. I brought you here to prepare you and I am going to send you back to tell your friends that there is a God. I want you to show them how to live for me. They will see Me in you."

By the time the sister finished delivering the message, I was sure God was speaking to me. I left the classroom and went to the dorm; I knew God was talking to me. I was scared. A guy from San Antonio was with Joel, his name was Ramon Martinez.

Ramon is now a Pastor in San Antonio. That day, he followed me to the dorm. I turned around to see him and I remembered him. I had chased him out of my mother's house before. He used to come around and practice singing with Joel. They had a gospel band together with other guys. When I realized it was Ramon, I started getting my things together. I didn't like him but he came in to hug me. I didn't want him to hug me. With tears in his eyes, he said, "You know that message was for you, Sonny. You don't know how much I have been praying for you. I know you don't love me but I love you and Joel and I have been fasting for you." He put his arms around me and gave me a sincere hug. When he did that, I saw another side to Christianity. I saw that even thought I treated him bad, he loved me. When he saw me leaving he started to cry again. He said, "I called your mother and she could not believe that you were here."

I saw a different kind of Christian, in Ramon, one who truly cared. I had not seen that before. I told him, "I have to go; I am going to be sick. I have to go to Mexico." Ramon said, "Sonny, if you get sick, I will take care of you." And he did. I had already started shaking, I was getting real sick. The withdrawals had begun and I was afraid to cross the border because they might have a picture of me since I was still a fugitive and because of the shaking and withdrawal symptoms, they would spot me right away. So I decided I would stay at the Bible School dorms just long enough to get past the withdrawals and then head down to Mexico for more drugs, or so I thought. While I was in the bunk, the students were all praying for me. The teachers knew that I was braking a heroin habit and going through withdrawals. This was not rehab center, they did not know about drug addiction but they did know how to pray and fast. Through the students, God showed me another kind of Christian. Every hour, in between classes, the students would come over to check on me. They would lay hands on me and pray for me. At night Raymond and Joel went out to buy olive oil so they could anoint me. They would take my socks off and anoint my feet and pray. I saw their love.

The other type of Christina had only judged me. This kind

of Christian only showed their love. I started praying and asking God for forgiveness because I had judged Christians the same. I was sick on Tuesday, Wednesday and Thursday. I ate nothing on those days, I couldn't. Friday in the morning I got up from bed for the first time and I went to the bathroom. When you go through withdrawals you don't eat, you just throw up. Everyone had gone to class. I got up and I was walking around when Raymond came in and saw me. He rushed over to hug me and started thanking God. He ran out of the dorm to the class and told them that I was up and walking. They all started to come to see me. Thanking God! They gave me things to eat and drink. They were all excited because of what God had done. Friday afternoon Joel invited me to go with him to a church service. I said, "No, I don't want to go." He said, "You will see other ex-drug addicts who have been changed by the power of God." I decided to see for myself. It was a very small church with crooked steps and located in the barrio.

People were lingering outside when we arrived. When we got out of the car, they started hugging us. I thought it was funny since they didn't know me. I sure felt out of place. Why is everyone hugging each other? I asked Joel, "What is this place?" He said, "It's a church." I said, "this isn't a church, I've never been to a church were everyone is hugging each other." Joel just said, "Don't worry; God is going to change you." I said, "I don't want to change that much." It looked a little like a gay club since I was seeing men kissing men on the cheek and so much hugging going on. I had never seen that before and I didn't want any guy coming to hug and kiss me. A big man came over to hug me and I just wanted to push him off. Joel wanted to sit up in the front. I still thought this was some kind of club. I saw them as wolves waiting to devour you. The men would get up to hug everyone that came through the door. I said, "Do you know them, Joel? Are you sure they are Christians?" He just smiled at me. I sat a little further back in the pews; Joel came to sit with me. The service was starting. It was Sonny Argonnzoni's Ministry and he was singing, "At The Cross." Now, it felt like a church.

The service started and the petitions had begun. It was a little

Set Free and Called

different, it was mostly testimonies. Then they made an altar call. Afterwards they started to preach. One man testified that he had been with me in Federal prison. The devil was telling me that he was a fake, that someone must have paid him to say that. Nick Cadena testified also, he was in Sonny Argonnzoni's rehab home and now he was a church Pastor. I said the same thing, this guy is a fake. I have never seen a drug addict change. I believe all these men were fakes. Nick was the one who made the altar call. He said, "If you think that I am a fake and that I am getting paid to do this then come to the front and God will show you that I am not a fake." He was reading my mind. Nick said, "I feel really bad because the devil is deceiving you. It is true. I serve God. I am not a "tecato" anymore. I serve here at Sonny Argonnzoni's ministry and if God brought you here tonight, come to the front and you will never be a drug addict again. He then said, "Stand up if you are ready to accept Christ." Something happened inside of me and I stood up." He asked us to come forward and I thought to myself, "I will fool him; I will walk toward the front and go the other way out." When I got to the aisle, I made a right turn but there were people going to the front and a big woman was standing in my way. I was face to face with her. You need to go that way; she said and pointed to the front. I got pushed to the front. I turned back to the altar. I was going through withdrawals during the service and I started getting very anxious. I got a strong pain right in the back of my head. This pain is caused by the withdrawals. It was like a shock that went from the head to my fingers. I got pushed back toward the altar. I wasn't ready to get saved. God was showing me some things but I wasn't ready. I was trying to figure out how to get to the back of the church but the people kept pushing me toward the altar, so I stopped. Nick Cadena kept looking at me and I kept looking at him. I wanted to see his eyes. I would know if he was hooked or high on drugs if I could see his eyes.

When I got close to the pulpit, he was repeating a prayer with the people. I was studying him and thinking, "this guy talks to much. I waved him over to me. He was wearing a real nice suit that night and I thought, "This guy is selling drugs, he is all dressed up and has real diamonds on." He must be getting paid pretty well; he must be working for the State. When he came over to me, I whispered, "Estas seguro que eras tecato?" (Are you sure you were once a drug addict?) He started to laugh. I asked him, "Do you have tracks? How long has it been since you used?" Nick said, "It has been over a year" and then he showed me the tracks on his arms. I asked him if they paid him to say all this. He just smiled at me and said, "So you are the one that thinks I am a fake, huh?"

I asked him, "How did you do it to get off the drugs?" Nick said, "It is God. Do you want to change?" I said, "Yes!" He said, "I won't even pray for you so that you know for sure that it is all God's doing. So go ahead and kneel." I kneeled at the altar and Nick said, "Now just start talking to God and ask Him to forgive you." All this time I was getting that strong pain at the back of my head. By that time, my mind could no longer cope. I didn't know if God was real or if He would forgive me so I said, "Look God, I don't know if you are real. I don't know if I am wasting my time here but I want you to show me that you are real." I was kneeling at this time. I got another sharp shock at the back of my head. I told God, "I have heard that you can do miracles. I need to believe you are real so take this shock from me and I will know you are real."

While I was talking to God, the piercing pain went away immediately. I told myself that the pain went away because of the way I was bending my arms and elbows, leaning on the altar. So I started to put my hands up; just stretching my arms to see if the shock had really left. It had! I kept my hands up and I started to believe in God. I said, "I know now that you are real, please forgive me." Tears started to roll down my eyes. I was embarrassed. I could not stop crying. I asked, "God please take the urge to do drugs away and I will serve you the rest of my life." My biggest desire was to stop the urge for drugs. The urge is what kills you. It is a big desire and addiction. The urge becomes your god, your mother, father and wife. There is no wife or family. The urge controls you.

When I got up from the altar, the urge had left me. The withdrawals were gone. I had an ulcer and could never eat very well but that night I got healed from the ulcer as well. I also had a hernia about an inch long. When God healed me that night, He healed all of me. The ulcer and the hernia and my addiction were all gone. I had never made the time to go to the Doctor to take care of myself but when I got up from that altar, I was a different person. I wanted to hug somebody. I started hugging people, complete strangers. Joel came up to me to hug me. He knew I had experienced a real transformation. When the service was over, Nick and Pastor Argonnzoni came over to talk to me. That night I learned a new vocabulary.

When I first saw Pastor Sonny Argonnzoni, he looked like a narc to me. He came straight at me and asked, "Where are you from?" I thought, "Man this guy is a narc." I said, "La Puente." He said, "Oh, no you aren't, you are from San Antonio." I said, "How do you know that?" He replied, "Your shoes, they are tangerine." He smiled at me and then he asked, "Do you have a place to stay? The reason I am asking is because we have a home." I questioned, "What kind of home?" He said, "It is my own personal home but I open the doors to people like you. I will give you a free room and free food if you enter our program. Want to try it?" I asked him, "What are you going to charge me?" I got suspicious and thought there must be a catch; nothing is free. He just smiled at me and put his arm around me. He spoke Spanish the entire time, he is Puerto Rican. I told him that I did not have a place to stay and that I would like to try the "Victory Home". Sonny Argonnzoni said that I couldn't have a car at the home so Joel took my car. The Pastor told Joel not to bring me the car for at least a month. Freddie Garcia and Carlos Moreno were also at the home at this time. They are both Ministers today.

At Pastor Argonnzoni's Victory Home, I saw a different kind of Christian. The Christians here were different from the ones I grew up with. These Christians wanted to give and to serve. They gave me a bunk bed and served me coffee. The Christians I had known would not give me the time of day. I believe God sent me there to know what Christians are supposed to be like. It was like training for me. God was teaching me about Christianity and His love. I started to see God's love in these people. Up to now, I had seen more love in the world than I had received in church. This rehabilitation program had a different kind of people. These people were not the same. They dressed different too. They had long hair, jeans, dressed very casual. They had beards. The other Christians were clean cut. In these long haired people, I saw love and real caring. They waited on you and loved you much more than I could imagine. I saw them praying for their food. I would cry when I would hear them praying because it was a simple prayer from the heart. I knew they loved God and their fellowman. The other type of Christians used eloquent prayers and was highly intellectual. Their prayers came from the head and not the heart. These people gave thanks for their food and prayed for all people in the streets who did not have a place to stay.

The first night there my bed was made for me and the guys checked on me. One brother came to my bed and knelt down He started praying, a very simple, heart-felt prayer for me. He was thanking God for my being there. Nobody had ever wanted me. He touched my heart because he wanted me there. He asked God to keep me there and not to let me leave. Then another brother came to pray for me, by this time, I was praying too. He made the same type of prayer. That night I don't even know if I ever slept but I had such a beautiful feeling inside that I did not want to lose. That same night, God called me into ministry. I saw myself in prisons. The whole night I saw myself behind a pulpit, preaching to others but I was behind bars; I was preaching to prisoners. For a whole month, I had that same vision but I did not really understand it. I was afraid to tell someone about it because I was still a fugitive. I couldn't stand it anymore. I thought God was telling me to turn myself in and go to prison for what I had done. I thought God was telling me that because I was a fugitive, I could not serve Him that I had to go to prison instead. I did not know God then; I could not discern that the devil was talking to me. It is good to have a Pastor to talk these things over with. Your own Pastor can answer your confusing thoughts and difficult questions. I started packing to give myself up to the Police. I now know that it would have been the worst mistake for me. The devil had a plan for me and that was to keep me behind bars for the rest of my life. I told one of the men at the Victory Home that I was packing to leave and he said, "Don't go until you talk to Pastor Argonnzoni first."

That night we went to the church service and after the service, I talked to Pastor Argonnzoni and told him I was leaving. I told him the whole story about my vision and he told that it was the devil's plan and that if I left; I was falling straight into his trap. He said, "Stay in the program, God knows you are here and if He wants you in prison, He will send the Police to come pick you up." "But what about the vision, what does it mean?" I asked the Pastor. He said, "It is God calling you into ministry, God wants you to preach in the prisons, He doesn't want you to turn yourself in. He is calling you to work in the prisons and be a minister. All you have to do is say "YES" to God, from then on, you will see how God begins to talk more with you." I replied, "I don't know anything about the Bible and about preaching." Pastor Argonnzoni said, "It is not going to happen right now, God just wants to know if you are willing. He is letting you know that your ministry will involve you going to preach in the prisons. Just say yes to Him and you will rest and God will take over." So I said yes to God and I went home. I started to pray. The brothers had taught me to pray and to give thanks to God for the whole day. I had been getting trained. So I prayed and told God yes and I rested. I no longer had the same dream. I told God that He would have to train me, prepare me and teach me first before asking me to do any preaching.

God knew all that already but I was praying to Him that way anyway. There was a guy named Ernie Aragones and one day about a month later, he came by the home for a visit and he was on his way to Chino prison farm. He wanted to take two guys from Victory Home to accompany him. He wanted to take me and even though I was a fugitive, I went any way. When I got there, there were about five guys from my barrio in San Antonio which had belonged to the Ghost Town gang. When Ernie gave me the pulpit, I did not know what to say so I gave a few words of gratitude to God for changing my life and I broke down crying. The devil began to tell me that they would laugh at me because I was crying. I found out later that the guys also broke down crying, they had been touched by that. Ernie preached a sermon and after the service I called Ernie to pray for my friends from San Antonio because I did not know how to pray properly for them. Ernie said to me, "God wants to give you stars for your crown which you will get when you get to heaven".

I later understood that this was all in God's plan since Ernie arrived at Victory Home and was asking for volunteers to go with him to Chino prison he looked at me and said, "I want to take you." I should not have agreed since I was a fugitive and could have been arrested, but instead of saying no, I agreed to go without hesitation before I realized what I was saying. I didn't know how to testify so I was a little nervous. Ernie told me on the way to the prison that God had told him to take me with him. I now see that God was training me. After that I kept going with Ernie to Chino Youth Training Camp and Corona Prison.

I was still a fugitive but since I had that dream of me going to prisons, I began seeing it come to pass. It was only six weeks since I had dreamt that dream and already I was going to prisons and talking to them about Christ. I started going to Tehechapie and San Quentin Prisons. God started using me to lead prisoners to Christ, to break the chains of addictions, low self-esteem and violence in their lives with my testimony. After those dreams became my reality, God began calling me to go to Bible School and get understanding of His Word and principles. I started to get a desire to learn the Bible. I met a black man on the streets, all the home residents went out to work in the streets and by this time, I had been saved for four months. I didn't know the Bible or how to testify but I would give out tracks and literature about the forgiveness and love of Jesus Christ. A black wino was sitting by the bus station and I sat near him and gave him a bible tract. I started talking to him about God. He had a big bottle of wine and he

Set Free and Called

said to me, "Which one; God the Father, God the Son or God the Holy Spirit?" He started to give me a bible study right there on that bus bench. He knew that the Father had sent His Son to die on the cross for us and that the Holy Spirit was sent to teach and guide us. He would take a drink in between and then continue talking about God. So after he gave me a full introduction about the three Gods, he said, "Now, which God do you want to talk about?" He embarrassed me because he was a wino but he knew the bible better than I did. But that was all part of God's plan so that I would be encouraged and committed to learning His Word.

I told the wino that I did not know about the three Gods but that I used to be a drug addict and that God had changed my life and delivered me from my addictions to heroin and alcohol. I said, "I don't know which one changed me but one of them did. I know one of them is living inside of me because now I am a new man. I am completely different than before. I don't have to shoot up anymore, I don't have to drink alcohol anymore and I know that He can do the same for you. Why don't you come with us?" And he did, he came into the Victory House rehab program and he gave his life to Christ that night. He went through withdrawals, like all of us, but the guys at the home served him and took care of him and when he was healed, he started teaching. It turns out that he had been a Pastor in Atlanta, Georgia and had left the church and his wife and no one had seen him for a long time. About a week later, he got in touch with his family and after a week or so, his entire family showed up to visit him. He told us his story that he had run away from God. He stayed with us about 3 months and then went home. I know that God used him to put a desire in my heart to learn more of the Bible.

When I was sure about going to Bible School, I realized that the school was very expensive and I was still living at the home. My wife, Lydia, was in San Antonio and she was ready to file for a divorce. I needed a push to make the right decision. I had a business in San Antonio and my father was pushing me to go back to San Antonio. He had not seen me saved yet but he wanted me to go to work. He could not understand why I was living with so many guys and he could not understand why none of the men had a regular 9-5 type of job. He would say; "If you are saved, why don't you work? Why doesn't every man at that home have a job?"

I would respond by saying, "Father, it is a Christian rehab home and we are doing God's work." "But how do you support yourself?" was his reply. He had so many questions and nothing made sense to him. He was a hard-working man, always working by the sweat of his brow and the lifestyle of the rehabilitation home was not commonplace in the early 70s. My father would then ask me, "Do you have a Pastor? What does he say about not working?" I would tell him, "Yes, we have a Pastor and he was a drug addict also." He would then say, "Well now I've heard everything, why do you want a Pastor that is just like you? Find yourself a Pastor who hasn't been on drugs."

I had this burning desire to go to Bible School but there were conflicting circumstances all around me with my wife, family and business. I did not know which way to turn. I asked my Pastor, Sonny Argonnzoni and he said, "God told me to tell you that He wants you in Bible School. Has God told you the same thing?" I said, "Yes, I have a desire to go but I have some problems. First I don't have any money and secondly I am living in the home." Pastor Argonnzoni replied, "You don't have any problems, leave it to God, He will work it out." He further said, "Tell God yes, that you will go to Bible School and let Him work out your problems. God knows you don't have any money. God knows where you are living and every other detail of your life. He knows you are in a program at this home and that you have a wife and a family and even with all your problems, God still wants you." God gave Pastor Argonnzoni a lot of knowledge and wisdom.

So I prayed and told God, "Yes, I will go to Bible School!" But there was still another problem which was a rule at the school. The rule was that you had to be saved at least one full year before you could enroll. I told Pastor Argonnzoni and he said, "Don't worry, if God wants you there, He will open that door. God also knows the rules at Latin American Bible Institute at La Puente, California."

Set Free and Called

The following Saturday, Joel came to the home to visit me. On Sunday we drove to LABI and I ran into the Bible School Superintendent, Brother Torres. He was really happy to see me and asked me immediately, "Are you going to Bible School?" I said to him, "I want to attend but your rules state that I need a letter because I have only been saved for four months." He replied, "I know when you got saved, Sonny, we were all there, remember? Go to the office right now and tell Sister Becky to give you an application and fill it out." I went straight to the office and found Sister Becky but she was telling me all the reasons why she could not give me an application. As that was happening, Brother Torres walked into the office and said, "Give him an application." I filled it out and brought it promptly back to her and she said, "That will be ten dollars please, that's your application fee." I did not have any money in my pockets so I said to her, "I don't have it right now but as soon as I do, I will give it to you." Just as I was saying that, Brother Louie Cruz, a student at the school, walked by and handed me ten dollars and said, "God told me to give you this offering." I took the ten dollars and gave it to Sister Becky with a smile.

It truly must have been God's idea because Louie was known to be a "tightwad" but even so, God used him to supply my need at that moment.

Then Superintendent Torres waived the requirement for a letter because he was an eye-witness of the miracle that God had done in my life. So as Pastor Argonnzoni has said, that door was opened and I was ready to attend Bible School when it started.

That following Sunday when I went to church, Pastor Argonnzoni called me to the altar. During the service the Pastor had asked for prayer petitions and I stood up in the congregation and mentioned my marriage that I wanted God to change my wife's mind about getting a divorce. I knew it was not God's will for us to get a divorce. One of her brothers was praying for a divorce and I was praying that God would intervene and prevent a divorce. When Lydia went to court to file the divorce papers, the attorney was sick and did not show up. Then at another time, the judge was in an accident and that hearing had to be rescheduled as well. In the meantime, my mom talked to Lydia and told her that it wasn't God's plan that we divorce. At the altar that Sunday, Pastor Argonnzoni said, "Tonight, you are going to hear from your wife." I never received calls from her. She did not believe that I had been saved. She had distanced herself from me and just wanted to divorce me and be done with the painful life I had put her through up to that point. Well, to my amazement, she called me. I told her that I was in a rehab home and that God had changed my life and that I loved her and did not want to get a divorce. She said, "After ten years and now that I am filing for a divorce you finally say to me that you love me? Sonny, I know what you are doing. I have heard there are drugs in California that people use to make love."

I said to her, "Lydia, I love you and God bless you." She thought I was just playing around; she did not expect me to say those things. She called my mother right away and told her that I had said I loved her and blessed her and she said she did not believe my new vocabulary. She had never heard me talk like that before. My mother said to her, "He is saved now, he is a new man." Lydia still did not believe; she just kept bringing up all the past and all the terrible things I had done before. My father then came on the line and said to her, "Lydia, you have been praying and fasting for Sonny to change and now that he has, you do not believe?"

CHAPTER EIGHT

The New Home

> "*The thief does not come except to steal, and to kill and to destroy,* **I have come that they may have life and that they may have it more abundantly.**" John 10:10

PASTOR SONNY ARGONNZONI called me to the altar and said, "Stand up, God just told me that tonight just before midnight, you are going to hear from your wife." When I got to the home, we had dinner and prayer. We went to sleep and about midnight, the telephone rang in the home. Nobody was supposed to use the telephone but our Home Director had stepped out so when the phone rang, a brother picked it up. He came to my room saying, "Someone wants you on the phone." I knew right away it was my wife and that God was causing this. The word that Pastor Argonnzoni told me earlier came instantly to my mind. He said, "Just before midnight" and it was a few minutes before midnight. He also said it would be my wife and sure enough, it was, it was Lydia calling me and she was at the Los Angeles airport. She wanted me to come pick her up. I was shocked! I did not expect her and I also had a problem since the Rehab Home I was living in had rules and one of them was that no one was allowed to go anywhere, especially not in the middle of the night. I had a new car at the home that I could not use except for ministry errands or to go to school. I told her I would pick her up but in my excitement, I forgot to ask her for the flight number or the name of the airline. She was calling from a pay phone so I could not just call her back.

I did not know Los Angeles or LAX at all. I was in a hurry to get to her but I had to get permission to go. Freddie Garcia was there and he was one of the Home Directors at the time. I told him that my wife had called and that she was at the LAX and she wanted me to pick her up. He questioned me about using the phone and I told him what Pastor Argonnzoni had said to me during the service. He said, "I have to take you." We get into the car and head straight to the airport. He asked, "What flight?" as we were walking into the huge airport. I told him I did not know so we went and had her paged. Lydia had already landed and was somewhere at that airport but we were not even sure which terminal. Freddie and I were walking around the airport and ran into some drug addicts. We had a whole bunch of tracts with us and I gave the men some tracts. I knew some of them from San Antonio and they could not believe it was me and that I was no longer a drug addict. We were trying to talk them into coming to the Rehab Home. In the meantime, I was playing around with one of the men who thought I was faking the whole thing. So I was laughing with him because I told him that I thought the same thing when I first met Sonny Argonnzoni. I thought he was a fake too. So we were laughing together.

Just at that very moment, Lydia passed by and saw me. When I looked at her, she started to cry. I asked her, "Lydia, why are you crying?" She said, "Because you are saved!" I said, "I told you I was; do you believe me now?" She replied, "Sonny, I really did not believe it until now." I asked her, "Why do you believe me now?" and she said, "Because you never used to smile or laugh like that, you look and sound totally different. I believe now that you are a changed man."

I had been so bitter and hard-hearted that I had not realized

The New Home

I never laughed or smiled. She was convinced now that I was saved and that God had changed me from the inside. She then told me that my father had given her a round trip ticket to use just in case she came and saw for herself and was not convinced that I was truly a new man, saved by the power of God. My father had advised her to see for herself and if I wasn't truly saved and changed completely for her not to stay with me. Lydia was so happy, she wanted to call my father right away and tell him the good news but I told her to wait until the morning. She insisted that my father would be waiting on the call and that she needed to call him right away so we found a pay phone for her to make that call. I wanted to hear that conversation so I stood nearby. She said, "He looks so different, he is smiling and laughing, I've never seen him so happy. He's gained some weight and his skin doesn't look so pale anymore. He looks really good and I am sure now that he has given his life to God and he is a new man." My father wanted to hear all that as well and now everyone could sleep better so we went to the home.

I did not know what I was going to do now. I wanted my wife and two sons with me. I had prayed that God would restore our family but I was living in this Rehab Home for men, going to Bible College and now I have my wife and two kids with me. My mind kept going toward getting a job to take care of them. When we arrived, the men at the home had prepared a little room for us with two bunk beds, one of them we used for Jesse and Mike, my two sons, and the other was for me and Lydia. We were happy for the first time in a very long time.

In two conversations over the phone, I had told Lydia to leave everything behind in San Antonio and come to Los Angeles and we would make a new life for us. One of the reasons, she wanted a divorce was because she had caught my oldest son, Jesse, playing as if he was a drug addict and giving himself a fix. She had put up with me and my crazy and dangerous life for a long ten years but when she saw this, it really affected her and she thought that if she stayed with me, our sons would become drug addicts also. Before I left for California, Lydia had started to change toward me. She did not want to be around me anymore. If I was in the house, she would go outside. She did not know what to do around me; she did not want to even be in the same room with me because of the cigarettes, the drugs, the life I was living and the man I had become. When I left for California, she was happy that I was gone. After receiving Christ into my heart and when she told me that she wanted a divorce, I told her that I was a new man and I wanted her to leave everything in San Antonio behind her and we would start a new life in California. She had no intentions of doing that because she thought I was still dealing and addicted to drugs.

In San Antonio, we had our own home and business but we ended up giving everything away, even the furniture. She was in love with her house and her furniture. She took great pride in them. We had the best and she was crazy about her house and everything we had filled it up with. I told her, I had made up my mind to stay in California and I asked her to leave everything behind and a start fresh new life with God in the center of our family. Encouraged by my father to come and see for herself, she came to California and she was so happy to see that I was a changed man but when she saw the little room that all four of us were in, she did not want to stay. I had a problem, a big problem.

I would tell her, "Do you love your material things more than God? If you give up everything for God, He will give you more, just trust in Him." After ten years of being saved, she did not believe, she did not have faith. She only knew the drug addict that had mistreated her so much, she didn't know the new man that was standing in front of her. She did not understand how I could have so much peace. We had so little, yet I was at total peace about it. She would say to me, "You have trailers and trucks in San Antonio and others are making money with them and here you are with nothing. You do not even have money in your pocket. You have never been without any money in your pockets. You have always looked for a way and here you are doing nothing but going to school. I don't understand, Sonny, I don't see how God is going to give us what we need." Lydia did not understand but neither did I but God was preparing us with great faith. In the past, I would always figure out my bids for my jobs, I was always looking for ways to make more money.

Now, that entire income stream was gone. Lydia wanted me to go to work. She said, "If I stay, you have to find a job. How can you be at peace about this, Sonny, you have never even wanted to live with anyone and here we are living with all these other men in the same house." She wanted us to have our own house and our own furniture. She would complain saying, "I don't even have a kitchen, no drawers, we are living out of a suitcase. Can't you see that we don't have anything?" She now wanted the "old" man and what he had provided for her. She would cry at night because she couldn't understand and I didn't understand how I was going to give her the things she wanted but I knew that God would provide one way or another. She would make me feel bad when she would say, "We are going down, instead of going up, instead of gaining; we are losing." I would try to comfort her and all the time I would pray to God for some direction and some answers.

I had fallen in love with God and I trusted him completely but to make my wife happy, I told her that I would look for a job and then we would get a house. So I had to make arrangements with the home to get permission to go out and work. They told me that it wasn't God's plan for me. The Director had a meeting with me and Lydia and said that if I left the Rehab Home, I would most likely go back to drugs. They told us that we should be in the home at least a year before attempting life on our own so that I could get a solid and godly foundation and strong support system. That day during the meeting the Director told us that the devil was trying to get us to give up and leave the plan of God. He reminded me that I had a calling on my life and that God would work everything out to our greatest benefit. Lydia got mad at the Director that day. She said, "We are not used to living like this. We are not used to living like tramps." She did not realize that if I life, I would surely end up back on drugs. The Director said, "Okay, go look for a job but if the calling is truly of God, you won't find a job, no matter how much talent you have, Sonny, God won't open that door."

So we left his office and I began looking for work, thinking that I would be able to find something right away. I would buy the newspaper every single day and find lots of jobs listed that I was qualified for. I was a good mechanic of cars and trucks, I was a certified welder, I would call and go to the jobs but before I got there, the job would be taken. I couldn't find work. So after a few weeks, I wanted anything. I wasn't going to be picky at all; I just wanted to begin to start making some money. But I could not get a job. Lydia called my father because he was making money with trucks that I owned so that he would send money for rent so we could at least rent a house. She was getting anxious and was ready to leave that Rehab Home; she wanted a place of her own.

So my father agreed to send money for three months to pay for rent until I found a job or started a business. My father was thinking that I would begin a business with my trucks in California but God had taken that desire of making money out of me. Lydia really wanted out of that Rehab Home and that little room we were all living in. I was faithful in looking for a job. Jobs pay very well in Los Angeles and I was a really good welder since I was very young but I could never secure a job. I also was very consistent about looking for a house to rent and many were for rent but each time we would get there, they would have rented it out to someone else or I would tell them that I was going to Bible School and they would decide not to rent to us. I had a brand new car; money was always there to make the payment. I would do little jobs here and there and God would always provide. So God was supporting us, providing for all our needs. My love for God grew and my love for Lydia also grew. I started to love her. I had never loved her before.

We could not rent a house and I could not find a job so I finally told Lydia, let's go home. I called my Dad and he was very happy to hear the news. He had just received a new contract for a large job and he could use my help. So we put everything we owned into the fastback mustang. So we were packing up when one of the deacons saw that we had everything in the car. I did not want to say good bye to Pastor Argonnzoni because I felt like a

The New Home

failure. I knew deep inside that I was making the wrong decision.

I went to the bathroom to pray. I was crying and telling God, "You know I have a family and you also know that I love you and want to do your will. I love this new life you have given me but I also have to take care of my family. If you would only help me just a little instead of closing every door I knock on. That tells me that you do not want to help me. I am not asking you for money, Lord, I gave up my trucks, drugs, house, furniture and my car. I gave it up for you. Now I have to go back to San Antonio because I cannot take care of my family here and I will look like a failure because I trusted you. They will laugh at me. I trusted you completely and gave everything up for you. Please make a way for us to stay here so that I can finish Bible School and I can finish what you have asked me to do. I know I have talent but yet I can't find a job anywhere. Why have you closed all the doors?" I felt like God had turned His back on me. I asked for forgiveness even though I didn't know why. I was just pleading with Him and trying to understand.

I was in the bathroom really crying my heart out to God, I was brokenhearted. I felt like I was not even asking for much, just a decent job to take care of my family and God was not providing that for me. Thoughts had even entered my mind that I had it much better when I was serving the devil. Lydia and my two sons were waiting for me outside in the car, they were ready to leave. The deacon, Bob Hernandez, thought we were going to wash clothes and asked me, "Did they let you go do laundry?" I left the bathroom with anger against God so I replied hastily, "No, we are going to San Antonio." He asked with great surprise, "Why, because you have not found a job?" I retorted back, "Yes, because I haven't found a job or a house for us." He replied very excited, "Sonny, I have a house for you but it will not be ready until Monday!" I was so happy to hear that because I wanted to stay and I wanted to believe that this was God's doing.

That was a Friday evening so we decided we would wait until Monday. We unpacked the car and went into our little room again. We had rent money and we believed that we would get the house on Monday so we testified on Sunday in the church service that we had a house for our family and everyone in the church gave us a standing ovation. We were very happy that weekend and everyone was praying for us. On Monday, Bob took us to go see the house and to talk to the owner. The landlady told us that the house had been rented over the weekend. We were depressed and I was mad with God again. I told God, "I know you are not for me, here I am testifying and witnessing over the weekend about how good You are but You won't let me rent a house for my family." When we got into the car and started going back to the Rehab Home, Lydia started all over again. She said, "You know that we are meant to be in San Antonio." I replied in anger, "OK, let's pack up and go home." Our intention was to leave as soon as we arrived. We were just going to get our things and leave but there was a big commotion going on. The Home Director had apparently slapped a young fifteen-year-old girl who was visiting one of the residents after she began cussing at him. She was using the phone when the Director asked her not to and she turned around and hit him on the head with her purse and started cussing at him so he slapped her. In the struggle, her blouse was somehow torn. The resident who had invited this young girl for a visit ran to the kitchen and grabbed a butcher knife and went after the Director. I saw that he was going to stab the Director so I grabbed him and took the knife away from him. The police were called and they took a report. I was mentioned in the report as saving the Director's life. This delayed our leaving to San Antonio because I was told by the police that I needed to be available as a witness. We decided to stay another day. The Home Director was given notice by the Board that he had to leave. The Board then gave all the men living in the home notice that they were going to close the home because they had no Director. The men started to leave that night about five or six men left right away. The next day, more left. In the meantime, I had to stay because I was a witness to the incident involving the Director and one of the residents. So we stayed another three days. The Board had a meeting in the living room so I went to our little room. The meeting was with the Director and they gave him a

The New Home

certain number of days before he had to be completely gone from the premises. If they did not let him go, the Board was worried that someone might file a lawsuit against the Ministry. Lydia and I were in our room when someone called me out, they wanted to talk to me. I was told that I had to leave because they were going to close the Rehab Home and rent the house. I was given ten days to leave. When I went to my room, I heard God say, "Ask them if you can rent it." So I did, I asked, "Why don't you rent it to me?" They asked me, "Do you know what this house rents for? It is $650.00 per month." Back in 1969, that was quite a bit of money for rent. They asked me, "Do you have that kind of money?" I replied, "Yes." They then said, "Well, when the Director leaves, we will talk again." When the Director left, the Chairman of the Board came to talk to me and asked me if I had the money to rent the house. I replied confidently, "Yes." I did not have it, but I said yes anyway. He then said, "We have agreed to give you the first month free but after that, you have to pay $650.00 the first of the month, do you agree?" I gladly said, "Yes, I agree." So Lydia and I ended up with the house and everyone else left.

About ten days later, one of the Board Members came by and there were ten guys in the home and he asked me, "How are you feeding them?" I said, "God will provide." The following week, another Board Member came by and we had more guys living in the home and he gave us an offering. When the thirty days were up two Board Members came by and by then we had twenty ex-drug addicts who had given their lives to Christ living in the home and we were having church services and bible studies. We also had one of the guys from the church picking up donations for us and we had a freezer, hamburger patties and French fries. So when they arrived they asked me if I had the rent money and I said yes. I did not have it but I intended to borrow it. One of the Board Members tells me that they had a meeting and they decided to give us three months' free rent. After three months, the Board Members drop by for a visit again and there were forty guys in the home and more food. We had secured Vons Super Market as one of our sponsors. They would give us truckloads of food. The Board

Members came back saying they were sorry that they had broken up the home and they wanted to come back as the overseeing Board and take over again. I said yes, I was glad to receive them, so they made me Home Director. They did not put any pressure on me in running the home because they saw that the Holy Spirit was directing my decisions and prospering the work. They were in agreement with everything I did. I never argued with them and they never argued with me.

After being there one year, they would take me to their churches and they would pick up large offerings for me and my family and the home. When we had been there one year, the owner of the house was in Joplin, Missouri and he came to visit us and gave us the house outright with all the furniture, wall to wall carpet and everything in it. He was a Pastor in Joplin. I had never met him before but he gave me the house with one condition and that was that I should never sell it but instead give it to someone who did the same type of ministry.

I was attending Bible College and running a home with no steady job. I never did get a job. I was the mechanic of the Bible School and the Church. God always supplied our needs. During this time, I continued going to Bible College; I enrolled the men in the home who had accepted Christ and every day I would take ten to fifteen men to visit the bible classes I was taking myself just like I did when I went with my brother, Joel. From that time on, while I attended the Latin American Bible Institute in La Puente, California, I supplied them with food. I brought them milk, meat, fruits, bread and so much more. I graduated on June 5, 1973. My thoughts were to stay in California but Pastor Sonny Argonnzoni had already told me I was going to be on payroll as a minister. Just about that time, Dale Evans, the famous TV and Movie actress, got saved and she started coming to Victory Temple as a member and she donated 750 acres to Victory Outreach. The land was in Victorville and Dale Evans and Roy Rogers, her husband, owned their land in Apple Valley which was close by. Pastor Argonnzoni's plans were to send me to Victorville but there was nothing there at the time, just a mountain and desert. Dale

The New Home

Evans and Roy Rogers built a Chapel, a dormitory, large kitchen, basketball courts and a well.

I was planning on staying in California because I was going to Victorville and I would be on salary. Part of me wanted to stay in California because of the secure salary and also because it was already established and I would not have to be the one leading the ministry.

At the same time, God was talking to me and I had received a prophecy. God said that He had brought me to this place to get saved but that He was sending me back to San Antonio so that my family and friends could see the change in me and that I was to tell others about Him. Within three years, God gave me the same prophetic word three times. I knew there was no doubt that message was from God.

I was going through a spiritual battle with myself, my wife and the devil. Lydia did not want to go back to San Antonio anymore. She was happy and she still had some insecurity that I might want to return to my old lifestyle of drugs and women. I thought that if my wife did not want to go to San Antonio then it must not be God's plan for us because He does not like reparations. I prayed that God would convince Lydia of His plan for my life. Then one night, Lydia woke me up in the middle of the night and said, "OK, Sonny, if you really want to go back, I'll go." Finally, one day during the Christmas of 1972, we were on the road again going home to San Antonio to visit for the holidays.

CHAPTER NINE

God Calls Me Back to San Antonio

WE WERE HAPPY TO SEE OUR FAMILY. I looked forward to seeing everyone. I saw things much differently than when I had left. A brother in Christ and my brother-in-law, Joe Rodriguez, invited us to his home and he invited several people that night. We had all been raised in the church together but we had not really known God. He invited everyone so they could hear my testimony. That night God worked on all of them and they all made decisions for God. Today they are all in different churches, serving God. When I was talking with the people, I was giving them spiritual advice to go back to church. They said, "You know how it is in the church, they won't accept us." I replied, "Go to a bible-believing church." It was a noisy dinner party, yet I heard God's inaudible voice telling me, "They are like sheep without a Pastor." From that moment on, I started getting apprehensive because I had never liked the limelight; it was not in my natural personality to lead a congregation. I was comfortable with leading a home to shelter and rehabilitate addicts. I wanted to help the drug addicts but after I heard God's voice, my thinking began to change; I knew God was leading toward being a church Pastor. I had five months to graduate. I started talking about going back to San Antonio permanently and I started making those plans.

In the three years that I attended school, the majority of the students knew what they were going to do when they graduated. I was the only one, it seemed, who had not known until the end of my third year. The only voice I heard during those three years was the devil. He would say to me, "Your friends are overdosing and you don't love their souls. You don't really love souls, the souls are in the barrio and you should go there." But it was a trick of the devil. He wanted me to go to them so that I would not finish Bible College and become established in the Word of God. It sounded right but it was not God's plan. If I had done that before I was prepared by God, I am sure I would have ended up on drugs again. God always prepares the person before He sends them out to do His work. He prepared the disciples three years before they ministered, Moses was prepared for forty years in the wilderness and the Apostle Paul was prepared for fourteen years. God prepared me by showing me a different kind of Christian love. God renewed my mind. After four years, I had learned about God and I knew how to fight the devil and I had become wise to his schemes and tricks. My next problem was who I was going to give the house and the rehab ministry in California to. So I started praying and had the men in the home fasting and praying as well because whoever took the home and the ministry would also affect them directly. I had also asked the Bible School to pray and ask God what to do with the home. Shortly after that, I got the impression of a name and it was Nick Cadena. Nick was already directing a rehab home so I told God to give me confirmation by everyone being united in that decision. As it turned out, everyone was. One night, we went to a revival and although we were friends, I did not know where Nick lived. He had taken me under his wing when I first arrived to California. I had asked God to put Nick right in front of me so I could speak with him face to face. That night, I ran into Mike at the revival and after the service, I saw Nick as well. Nick had already heard that I was planning on returning to San Antonio so he had come to the revival hoping to find me. He asked me if it was true and I confirmed that I would be leaving for San Antonio and that I wanted to ask him to take

God Calls Me Back to San Antonio

over the home ministry. He leaped for joy and said that they had been fasting and praying to receive that home because they had thirty women who needed a place to live. I said, "Well, in three months I will be leaving and the place is yours." Nick would bring the ladies to lay hands and pray around the home for the next three months.

Before hearing from God to give the home to Nick Cadena, the devil tempted me to sell the house by saying, "You will need the money for the ministry. Selling the house is the wise thing to do." I had given my word to the previous owner of the house that I would never sell the home but instead make sure that it was always used for ministry. If I started breaking my word now, why stay in ministry?

After that decision was made, I just waited to graduate and slowly I started getting the burden for San Antonio and at the same time to open a Church. Pastor Argonnzoni and others tried to encourage me to stay in California so I prayed and asked for another confirmation. There was a revival in Long Beach and John Metzler was preaching and I wanted to hear from God. I went and sat up front on the first floor. My purpose was to hear directly from God. I did not want anyone to recognize me or speak to me because they knew me; I wanted to hear from someone who did not have any knowledge or information about me. I wanted God to confirm the thoughts that I was getting were from God himself. Lydia kept telling me the thoughts I had to go back to San Antonio were mine. Evangelist Metzler opened his Bible and then said he could not preach until he delivered this message first. He said that there was someone in the audience that God wanted to talk to. He said, "God says, the thoughts you have are Mine and cursed is the man who trusts in man." When he made the altar call, Evangelist Metzler was prophesying and I came to the altar and he looked at me and said. "You are the man God was talking directly to."

I went home and doubt still came to me and I wanted more confirmation. I felt like Gideon so I asked the Lord to please give me another confirmation that we should move to San Antonio and that I should open a Church. So the following night I went to the same revival with Evangelist Metzler but this time I sat in the balcony. I sneaked in so that no one would see me and I sat all the way to the back. I could not even see the Evangelist from my seat and I was sure he could not see me. He preached his message and when he made the altar call, he said, "There is a man in the balcony and God wants you to know that your thoughts are not yours, they are Mine, says the Lord and cursed is he that trusts in man." By this time, I was convinced that my thoughts were indeed God's instructions for us and all my doubts left.

I was almost ready to graduate. My graduation date was June 2, 1973 and my car was already packed. We were looking forward to going back to San Antonio. God had put a call in my heart and He had taken my fears away. I had been afraid that I might go back to drugs and I was also afraid to fail but all that fear was removed by God. Pastor Argonnzoni told me the day before my graduation, "I am giving you a leave of absence for six months. If this call is of God, you will see God moving in your ministry and doing things for you in six months. I will call you in six months to see how things are going. If you have to come back, I will send for you. If you do come back, I will send you to Victorville to oversee that ministry for us."

The graduation ceremony ended at 7:00pm but we were too tired to travel that day so we decided to leave early Sunday morning. We had our 1968 Ford Mustang hatchback loaded down with family and things. Riding in the car were Lydia, myself, our two sons, Jesse and Michael and our daughter, Liz. We were very tight but very happy. We pulled a 5x8 trailer behind us with our belongings.

Sunday morning at 10am, Lydia and I prayed again and said, "Father if this is not your perfect plan for us, stop us from going to San Antonio. We believe that you are guiding us and that you have another ministry for us in San Antonio. We want to ask you to forgive us if this is not you telling us to go. Every time we put a fleece before you, you have given us the word by prophesy and we have moved on that word. If we have heard you incorrectly, please stop us because we want to do your perfect will. If You are not with us, we will not get anywhere but if You are with us, I know we will be successful."

So we left and took the Santa Ana southbound in 100-degree weather without an air conditioner in the car, packed down with people, a single axle on the car and pulling a small trailer covered with a tarp. We felt like the Beverly Hillbillies. We took the Interstate 5 South to Riverside and then the Interstate 10 all the way to San Antonio, Texas. We ran about 100 miles, just before Indio, and as I was coasting downhill, I looked at the temperature gage and it was over the danger mark. The car was running super-hot! It happened at the exit with a garage so with the Mustang being a four speed standard; I let it coast toward the exit and into the garage. As we were exiting off the Interstate on the ramp, the motor locked but we continued coasting. When I stopped, I looked at the car and found a hole in the radiator hose. We left the car there to cool down a bit and walked over to a Denny's Restaurant with the family. We were able to stretch our legs and get a bite to eat at the same time. My wife and I prayed and gave thanks to God for stopping us from going to San Antonio. We were both thinking that this was God's way of stopping us from leaving since we had prayed that prayer before setting out that morning. I was thinking I would call Pastor Argonnzoni to come and get us. I was a mechanic so I was well aware that once a motor locks up the crankshaft is not good anymore. So I was pretty much convinced that we should head back to California.

After we ate, we headed back to the car and I was going to make that phone call so I began looking for Pastor Argonnzoni's phone number when suddenly I felt a strong urge to lay hands on the vehicle. I felt that God was telling me that He had NOT stopped us that it was the devil that had stopped us. "Tell the devil to get out of the motor" is what I heard in my mind. I told Lydia what I was feeling but she did not believe me, she was sure it was just a failed motor. Two hours had passed and the car was now cooled down. I put water in the radiator and I laid my hands on the hood of the car and I prayed and told the devil to get out of the motor. By sheer faith, I went and sat in the driver's seat, laid my hands on the steering wheel and started the car. The car started like a brand new car. There was no smoke at all coming from under the hood. So we drove to San Antonio with great boldness and confidence because for the first time, we were absolutely sure that we were in God's perfect plan and that He had a great ministry for us back home. We drove for another 24 hours or more and never had another bit of trouble with the car.

We are now in San Antonio and I am thinking, "Now, what God? How do we get started?" There were now five in my family so we did not want to stay with my parents, although we did stop by there for a visit when we arrived in town. The first one to visit me was Freddie Garcia and Javier Martinez. Both of them had been with me in the rehab home in California. Although God had already told me not to work with others, Freddie offered me a job. God told me He did not want me to depend on other men, that He alone would provide all that we needed. One night I felt the need to go and pray at a motel. I needed the privacy and quiet time before the Lord. My purpose was to fast and pray for direction from Him. I did not know where to start but I knew God would tell me. I told God that I was staying in that motel room until I heard from Him. I also told the lady manager at the motel front desk that I did not want to be disturbed. I told Lydia to go to Church and also ask everybody to pray.

I fasted and prayed for three days and three nights. On the third day, I was reading the Bible and fell asleep. While I was asleep, I had a dream that I was on Somerset Road and Palo Alto Road at the Grey Eagle Bar. I saw myself witnessing to many addicts and winos there, evangelizing and passing out Christian tracts. I woke up from that dream and started rebuking the devil because I immediately thought he was telling me to go back into my old life because that particular bar, the Grey Eagle Bar, was a major drug connection. I was wrong; God was giving me my answer and telling me which side of San Antonio He wanted me to work on. Freddie Garcia was on the Westside of San Antonio and God was now directing me to the Southside. After

God Calls Me Back to San Antonio

that dream, I prayed and went to bed for the night. That night I had another dream. In the dream, I was parked with my mustang in front of the Grey Eagle Bar. I was standing in front of my car door and it was opened. In front of me I saw an old man with long hair and a beard walking toward me. When he got to me, he starting pointing to my driver's seat and when I looked, all I could see was a pony tail. He just kept pointing to the pony tail and then he said, "Pull it." I pulled the pony tail and a young girl came out. When she came out, she was jumping joyfully, she was very happy. I looked at him and he had a smile on his face. He said, "I called you for this." Then he pointed toward the Grey Eagle Bar and said, "And I called you to them." Then I went inside the Grey Eagle Bar, I knew everybody there and when they saw me, they were astounded and their hairs stood up. I started witnessing to them. I started yelling and crying. They started screaming, like those screams I heard in hell. I was telling them that they did not have to be drug addicts. The dream ended while I was ministering to them.

It was about 3am and I woke up. I called Lydia right away to tell her the good news that God had spoken to me and told me where He wanted me to go. She was not happy at all, she started bringing up all the women in my past life and that the Grey Eagle Bar was my old hangout. "Esta bueno, Lydia, I am going to go get something to eat now." I hung up with my wife and started to pray. I said, "Lord, you have given me two dreams now so if this is really you telling me to go to the Southside, you convince Lydia." About 9am, I was getting ready to go pay for another night's stay when the phone rang and it was my wife. Lydia said, "Are you sure it was God that said the Grey Eagle Bar?" I replied, "Yes, I am sure." She then said that she had called my mother about the dream and my mother told her to pay attention because I was praying for an answer and God would definitely give an answer. So she then told me that she would go with me to the Southside. I replied by telling her that I would check out, pick her up and then we would drive to the Southside and look around. My mother had made some caldo [soup] for me so I broke my fast that day.

Lydia and I drove over to the Grey Eagle Bar. It was on a "Y" intersection. To the left is Somerset Road and to the right is Palo Alto Road. We stopped in front of the Grey Eagle Bar and prayed. I felt led to go to Palo Alto Road so we drove south just looking around. We thought that maybe we would rent a house that we could convert into a rehab home. We went under Highway 35 and just drove; relying on God to direct us. The first street had no stop light and there was neither a school nor a library at that time. We made a left and then we made a right onto Spaatz Street and drove all the way down that street. It was like a wilderness, we saw no people and no houses were built on that street at that time. At the end of the street, we saw a white tree that had a "For Sale" sign on it. We got off the car and walked around a bit. We had to watch out for snakes. We prayed again, because after seeing that sign, we now thought that maybe we could buy land and build something on it. The telephone number was on the tree so I wrote the number down. I put another fleece before God and said to Him, "I don't know how much the owner wants for his land but you know that all I have is seven hundred dollars. So if you want us to have this land, he will agree to seven hundred dollars and I will not have to argue much with him, he will accept it gladly. I am willing to give it all and have nothing left if this is where you want us to be. I will know it is you if he takes seven hundred dollars for this land." I wanted to be on the exact street where God wanted us to be.

We had lived on a street called Star Path in California so when we saw Spaatz Street, it kinda struck us. The "For Sale" sign had a phone number and also said, Coney Island on it. I drove to Coney Island and asked for the owner of the land. I asked him how much he wanted for his land on Spaatz Street and he said, fifteen hundred dollars. I was a little relieved because I really did not want to go there. It was raw land filled with cacti and brush and it would have been a lot of work to clean and build. I thanked him and I started to walk off. Lydia was waiting for me in the car. The little restaurant was empty and as I started walking out the man called out to me. "Oye, muchacho [Hey, young man], did

God Calls Me Back to San Antonio

you come here last year, you and two others, wanting the land for a church?" I walked back and said, "No, that wasn't me." He responded quickly and said, "It WAS you, the other two were ministers." I said, "No, you are wrong, no quiero faltarle respecto, pero he estado en California. [I don't want to disrespect you, but I have been in California]" He said, "Yo muy poco me equivoco. [I am seldom wrong] Do you still want to build a church?" I had told God in prayer that I would not say anything about building a church to the owner. I replied, "I want to do something for God. I want to work with drug addicts because I was a drug addict once myself." He said, "How are you going to work with them?" I said, "I am going to tell them about God." I really did not want to talk too much because I had asked God to do all the talking for me. He asked me, "How much do you want to give me for the land?" I said, "All that I have in my pocket, I have no credit, I have no job, no one loves me and no one helps me. I will give you everything I have in my pocket but that is all I have. He said, "How much do you have in your pocket. I said, "Seven Hundred Dollars." He said, "No, hombre, no es ni la mitada. [No Mister, that isn't even half]" I said, "It is all I have." I was about to leave when he said, "Do you have the money with you right now?" I said, "Yes!" Right away, he took off his kitchen apron and said, "Follow me." I followed him home, which was just around the corner. He lived with his daughter and he told her that he was selling the land. They argued because she was insisting on selling for fifteen hundred dollars. He eventually came out with the property deed and said, follow me to the notary public so we can make the transfer. We went to the notary public and the notary wanted fifty dollars. I did not have it. The owner of the land ended up paying the fifty dollars so he actually ended up with six hundred and fifty dollars for the land sale.

I wanted to purchase the land myself. I did not want to borrow from anyone. I used to con, burn and connive people in the past and I never paid anybody back when I borrowed from them so I did not want to take anyone's money, I wanted to do this on my own. I felt that no one would even trust me. So I was relying completely on God. I did not want any handouts, I had faith that God would provide for me, my family and the new ministry He was asking us to build. I told God, "As long as you support us, I will work for you. If you ever want me to quit the ministry, then all You have to do is stop providing for our needs." My brothers and my father had businesses and they offered me work but I had to show them that my God would supply our needs. To this day, I have that petition before God. In the ministry, the bills have to be paid and if one day there isn't enough to pay for our needs, then I know it is time for me to be retired and pass the mantle on. When my brothers offered me help, I felt they were testing me to see if I had really changed.

We obtained our first 50x100 lot on Spaatz Street that day. From that day on, Lydia would stay home with my mother and I would go every day to clear out the lot. The street in those days was not even a paved street yet, it was a city dump spot. There were mattresses, commodes, roofing material, you name it and it was dumped there. It was also a lover's lane since it was a deserted dead end. The addicts also came there to prepare their fixes. It was an entire city block and it was full of cacti, snakes and garbage. The cacti were 4 feet in diameter and every one that I ripped out had many snakes. It was also like a swamp, I had to put in fill dirt to even out all the low spots that collected rain water. I got a company who gave me free fill dirt and even leveled it for me. I cleaned about half of the lot and made a tent for myself because I did not have money for gas to go back and forth so I stayed in the tent to be near the addicts. I wanted to be near them so I could minister to them.

I could see the addicts that were doing drugs from my lot. They would go to the large house down the street to cook the powder and then they would come and sit under a tree. I would then walk over to them. At first they were afraid; they did not know who I was. After they got to know me, they learned to trust me. I was working on the lot, hoeing, when a brother-in-law dropped by. I had not seen him in a long while.

The last time I had seen him I had burned him for ten

thousand dollars. At that time, he had come from Chicago with ten thousand dollars and asked me to buy heroin for him. This was during the height of my drug days. I had told him I would send a runner or "mula" across the Mexican border to get it for him. Instead, I put the money in my pocket and never got the drugs for him. When he came back in two days for the heroin, I told my brother-in-law, that the runner had been stopped at the border and he had given his name, Genaro Rios from Chicago, as the person he was going to deliver it too. So I told Genaro, "You better go back to Chicago, the cops will be looking for you." So he left and went back and I had not seen him since. Ten thousand dollars was big bucks in those days.

It had been four years since Genaro returned to San Antonio and he never knew that I had burned him for that money. I eventually told him and I repaid him in various ways. His children came to school at my ministry for free. That afternoon, he asked me what I was doing on the land. He thought I was still in California. I asked him, "What are you doing here?" He said, "I have the two lots next to you. I came to clean them up since the City complains and fines the owners if the lots are not kept clean." He asked me, "How much did you pay for your lot?" I replied, "Seven hundred dollars." He said, "Do you want to buy mine?" I said, "Yes, but I don't have any money right now." He said, "I will give them to you and you can pay for them later when you can." I had a fleeting thought that maybe he knew that I had swindled him out of ten thousand dollars and he wanted me to build on his lots so he could take them back at some point. But I was wrong, he said, "I will give you the papers now and you can pay me later. We can go to the notary public now and do the transfer if you want. I did not even have money to pay for the notary's service. He said, "Don't worry; I will pay for the notary."

We had not discussed the price but we headed for the notary's office. He then told me that he had only paid four hundred dollars per lot and that was what he was willing to sell them to me for. So now I was getting two lots for just eight hundred dollars. That night I prayed and thanked God for providing more than

I expected. I now had three lots which were purchased free and clear with little to no money, no credit and no assistance from others. We had no electricity, no water but we had the land. I had a tent but no place for my family yet. The land was getting cleaned up but there were still snakes and cacti all around us.

One day my brother, Joel, called my father and said that his touring bus had broken down. He had converted a large commercial bus into a small apartment and he used it to travel with his gospel singing group as they ministered and evangelized throughout the United States and Mexico. His bus had broken down in Houston, Texas and my father wanted me to go to Houston to see if I could fix his bus. I went in my car and carried the tools I thought I may need. When I arrived, I discovered that the motor was locked. The bus had been driven without oil. I told him that we had to leave the bus for now since there was nothing we could do. It needed a new motor. Joel began taking his clothes, albums and equipment he had on the bus and loading into my car. We filled the car and still left a lot behind. As we were leaving a DPS officer pulled up and asked if we were leaving the bus there. The policeman said this is going to be a public hazard since it is on the edge of the road. If anything happens, you are going to be responsible. I advise you to get a wrecker and pull it off the road. Joel said, "I don't have any money right now but we will get someone to come from San Antonio and get that done. The Police gave us 24 hours to move it or get a large fine.

Joel and I got into my car and we began driving back to San Antonio. At some point, Joel turned to me and said, "Why don't I sell you the bus? How much money can you give me for it?" I told him, "I don't have any money right now." He just kept bringing it up over and over. He was convinced that I should buy the bus from him. He said, "All you have to do is pull it home and if you need money, Apa [Father] will be glad to lend you the money, you know he will." I said, "No, I am not going to borrow money from Dad or anyone else. God took me out of that life and I will not ask people for a loan. God will provide. He will make a way for us to have a house."

God Calls Me Back to San Antonio

When we arrived in San Antonio, I took him home. Joel was unmarried and still living with our parents at that time. That night I decided to stay at my father's house as well so that I could take a shower. I did that every other day or so since we did not have any running water on the lot. We walked in the house and after greeting everyone, I went straight to the shower. Joel started working on Apa, trying to get him to buy the bus for me. I heard him say, "Real cheap, Apa, just ten thousand dollars since it does not run and it needs a new motor." Apa was so good, he was going to give him the money for the bus, to buy it for me. When I came out of the shower, they were still talking and Joel had convinced our Father to purchase the bus for me. I quickly went over to them and said, "No, I do not want Apa to pay for the bus. I don't have any money to pay him back right now. I would rather live under a tree than go this route but I am not worried, I know God will supply." After Joel went to sleep, my Father kept after me wanting to give me the money for the bus but I just kept telling him that God would support me.

Two days went by and Joel still had not moved the bus from the side of the road so he came by the lot where I was clearing out brush and he said, "OK, if you don't want to buy the bus, why don't I lend it to you for six months while I find a buyer. You go get the bus and I will lend it to you for six months." I said, "I don't have a commercial truck to pull it." But Joel had already spoken to our Father and he had already agreed to lend me one of his 18-wheelers so that I could go get the bus from Houston. Apa had also already agreed to pay for the gas for the trip. So I agreed to accept Joel's offer and Apa wanted to come with me; so we set off to Houston.

Now God had provided a luxurious bus for us to live in. I brought my family to live on the bus and we were so grateful and thanking God, laying hands on the bus and praising God for His goodness toward us. We did not have any lights or running water and we had to fight off large mosquitoes but we were so grateful. We parked the bus in the corner of the land and we knew we would have it for at least six months or more. We knew that this was just the beginning of what God had prepared for us and although it was difficult and we had many struggles, we were confident that it would all work out better than we could even imagine. So, we kept on believing and kept on praying and claiming those promises and constantly relying on God's faithfulness to provide and guide us. I was also having trouble in school; problems just seemed to follow me. I started having more and more trouble with authority figures, the police, school teachers and principals, my pastor, my mother and father. I then started a gang in my neighborhood. We called ourselves the Ghost Tower Gang. During 1951, I lived in the barrio around 19th and Tampico Streets and there were very few schools for Mexicans. There were only two schools at the time, Lanier and Tech High Schools. We could not get into Lanier because it was full so we were sent to Tech but Tech High School had the teens from Casiano Courts, Ghost Town, Lake 24th Street, Las Colonias and Las Palmas Barrios but the gangs were closer to downtown, which was where Tech High School was.

In 1951, I went to Tech High School and the very first day, we clashed with our rival gang. A gang war broke out right in front of the Tech High School office. We were sent home and never even made it inside the school building. The police chased us and caught some of us. The second day we showed up more prepared with knives and chains but the police were ready too. There were policemen everywhere. That second day, they caught more of us and warned us that if we showed up again, they would send us to juvenile correction. Eventually the School also told me to leave and I was expelled from Tech High School when I was not even register. I came back two or three days later and was told not to hang around. Officially, I was never expelled since I was never registered in the school but my father received a letter thanking him for not sending me to that school. After that, I was in the streets but I always had a desire to make money because my father was a business man and even though I was only fourteen, I had dreams of being rich. My father did not want me to be hanging out in the streets, he wanted me to be educated but I couldn't because I knew that due to gang violence, I could be thrown into jail. My father and I fought all the time, he would force me to go to school but I would not go. Instead, I would pretend to go and just stay out all day long so my parents thought I was in school during the day. When my father found out, I left home because he also found out that I was using drugs and I did not want to hurt him, so I left the house.

After the incident at Tech High School, I graduated to using heroin. At first I started using one time only and then the following week, maybe twice that week and then I was using once a day and then it grew to two, three and four injections per day. That was just to be normal and have a normal day. I guess what bothered me most was that I knew I came from a good family. I saw the pain in my mother's eyes. I ran into her in the streets and she would ask for my forgiveness because she didn't know what she had done wrong to cause me to leave the family and use drugs. She came from a decent family and it was a shameful thing to have a drug addict in the family. I knew that I greatly offended my family not just because they loved me so much but because of their Christian beliefs.

In those days, it was not true Christianity, it was religiosity and very legalistic. My sins were considered a curse. By the time I was fifteen, I was lost and nobody wanted me. When I would go visit my friends, their parents would run me off. They would chase me off their properties with a broom.

Today addiction is not looked down as a curse or a sin, now it is looked on as an illness. They even give you free needles so you won't get AIDS and you don't spread it. But in the early 50's, if they found a needle in your possession or in your backyard, they would give you thirty years in prison. If you hid an addict from the law in your house, it was against the law. The law has changed since then. At that time, they did not know why people injected themselves with such deadly drugs.

So, young and wild, I left for Chicago with my cousin. We stole a car and went as far as La Mesa, Texas. We had no idea how to get to Chicago; we just knew that it was north so we went north. We were so stupid; we did not even know where Chicago was so we got to La Mesa in December completely unprepared for the trip. We were wearing nylon shirts in the middle of winter, freezing with no money and no gas. We quickly had no food to eat so we stopped at a gas station and a man offered us a job pitching bales of cotton. He paid us fifty cents which was just enough to buy gas to go to his ranch. We had not eaten so he gave us another fifty cents so we could buy some bread and Spanish peanuts and we made ourselves some burritos. We were so hungry. The next day, we worked hard on the Ranch. We slept in the car with no blankets and it was freezing. All we had were the nylon shirts with short sleeves and it was snowing outside. The man did not offer us anything warm. That afternoon, he paid us fifty cents an hour, which gave us enough money to go back to San Antonio and start all over again.

When we got back, we found out that the man who owned the car we had stolen was watching us and found the car right away once we got into San Antonio. He took his car back. A friend of ours stole another car for us because he wanted to go to Chicago with us so finally we started for Chicago again. This time we were a little more prepared, we took jackets and blankets and this time we had more money, enough for the trip.

I was fifteen years old and was not afraid of anything. My cousin's father lived in Chicago except that we did not have an address for him. We just knew that he was a wino and lived in the downtown area of Chicago where all the winos hang out. When we arrived in Chicago the first night, we slept in the car. We were told to search down Halstead and Madison Streets. The car broke down and we could not get it started. Chicago never slept; it was wide open at all hours of the night, the bars, stores and night life. In the morning, we went to eat at the local wino hangout and ran right into my uncle. I actually had two uncles there, one was my mother's brother and the other was married to my mother's sister. One was named Tony and the other Polo. When they saw us, they were very surprised. We were so young but Uncle Tony was happy to see his son who had traveled with us from San Antonio. He

God Calls Me Back to San Antonio

was happy but still got very angry with me for bringing his son on such a long and difficult trip. They were hung over but even so, he took his belt and started waving it at me and saying, "You are not this kind of person, you come from a Christian family. You shouldn't be here!"

They accepted me because I lied and gave them a sad story about my father. I told them that he abused me, beat me, made me work and took all my money. They felt sorry for me, so they kept me with them. They were homeless and lived in an abandoned building with no bathtub. They stayed warm by putting firewood and just broken pieces into a fifty-five gallon drum and lighting it on fire. That was their heat source during those brutal Chicago winters. My uncles begged for money so they could buy their wine but we were too proud, instead we stole. After a while, my uncles really liked us because we bought their wine. We started to steal from stores until my cousin started purse snatching and found there was more money in that. My cousin, Mike, stole one purse per day, as needed, until we started getting good at it and then we would work two or three together. We had a system worked out and stole purses for about six months. Chicago was bad, nobody cared to get involved. We finally were able to get an upstairs apartment and my uncles were happy because now we could take baths.

My friend, Jimmy, made a connection for marijuana so we started selling. We did not have to steal anymore. The landlady also owned The San Antonio Bar and we would keep an eye on the bar for her so she did not charge us rent. We did odd jobs and overall did what we wanted. The landlady liked us, she always had her eye on me and maybe she liked me because I worked hard. If she needed a bouncer, we were handy so she called us for help. I would also fix her car. I know now that God was in control of my life even then because He would send people to help take care of us. We always had money in our pockets. She would always slip me a twenty here and there.

We were at The San Antonio Bar for over a year and my mother and father didn't know where I was all this time. Nobody from San Antonio knew I was in Chicago. I suffered in Chicago because there was a loneliness and sadness inside of me. I missed my family and loved them very much yet I knew I couldn't live a Christian life. I just did not fit into their life. I would embarrass them so I really did not want to be there. I felt like I did not fit in at all. I had food, lodging and money so for now, I was okay. I believe the Lord used the landlady to help care for me like a mother. It was some kind of a home. We would talk and I would do errands for her. I never charged her yet she would always pay me. The bar was always full, even though it was a dangerous place; God gave me a place to live. It was hard to rent an apartment at age fifteen, but God made it possible. I had money for clothes, I was always clean and now I know that it was God's hand of grace and protection upon me all those years. The landlady would ask me if I needed anything such as ironing, even though she knew we were thieves and sold drugs. She still trusted me behind the bar, where she had a lot of money in her cash register.

Finally someone told my father that I was in Chicago and instinctively, he knew exactly where I was. He came to Chicago and to take me home. We had a long talk. I told him I did not want to embarrass them but my father said that it did not matter for me to come home anyway. He was crying because I did not want to go with him. I just didn't want to hurt them or make them a laughing stock because of me. He said, "I will put you to work in my business."

While I was in Chicago, I would spend the day at Ocean Drive and would sometimes see the Army recruiting officer. But when I tried to enlist, the recruiting officer laughed and said, "You're only sixteen years old and you only weigh 108 pound, go home!" I told my father that I wanted to enlist in the Army. His response was "No, you'll get killed!" Once we got back to San Antonio, I tried enlisting in the Military again but this time in the Navy. They rejected me because of my age and weight again. On my way, I saw the Army Air Corp and walked into their office and said I want to enlist. They said, "Yes, but you need to bring your father and he has to sign." I told my Father and after much discussion about it, he agreed to sign for me since he knew that I would go back to Chicago if he did not help me enlist.

I signed up for active duty in 1952 for a total of four years. I took my basic training and most of all I wanted to go to the frontline. I wanted to see Korea and Japan. I wanted to see the world. I had plans and dreams to go to war. I was very young and did not use my head but God had other plans. When I finished basic training at Lackland in San Antonio, Texas, I realized that I was right back where I started, in my home town again. I felt like I was just moving in circles when all I wanted was to see the world. Kelly Field proved to be good to me. The Army Air Corp sent me to school and I was able to get my G.E.D. Soon it was 1956 and the war had ended but I had gotten worse, my behavior had not improved. I had picked up even more vices.

My purpose for joining the Military was to go to war. Everyone else was afraid but not me. I wanted to fight, I wanted to travel. I didn't think about loyalty to my country, just getting out and doing what I wanted. The recruiter told me I would see war and that I would see the world. No one at the Lackland Training Center wanted to go because men were getting killed. The training officer would tell us you have two months then he would say, you have one month, he wanted to make sure we were trained right so we could defend ourselves. Every time I talked to my buddies, they would tell me I was crazy because I wanted to go to war. In my squadron there were more than 300 men and only one third made it through the training. They were either too fat, had heart problems or just didn't pass. Some would faint and the ambulances would come pick them and they were never seen again. Graduation Day was Beer Party Day, everyone was crying with their buddy. We had developed friendships and we knew we might never see each other again. The Drill Instructor gave us his blessing saying, "may God have mercy on all of you." After that all night party, many were passed out. It was a time of love and unity even though we only knew each other for three months. We hugged each other and held each other like little kids because we knew that many would not make it back.

The next day, the Sergeant came with orders for everyone which included a 15 day furlough. He started calling out names, everyone got their orders except me. I was left alone in the barracks. I did not know what was happening. A couple of days later, I found out. The Commanding Officer called me to his office and asked me, "What are you doing here, son?" I thought to myself, "Don't you know?" He continued, "you are too young, you should be in school. I am not going to send you to Korea." I felt bad, I really wanted to go and I told him so. He said, "No one wants to go to war, what is the matter with you? Are you crazy?" He began checking my records and saw the name of my recruiting officer and said, "I am going to have a talk with your recruiting officer, you should not be here." But all I could say was, "I want to go to war!" He said, "No, if I send you; you will get killed for sure, you are just a kid!" I replied by saying, "No, I am a man!" I wanted to tell him that I had been around, I had gone to Chicago on my own and taken care of myself but I didn't. He said, "Look, son, you think you know what is best but I am going to send you to school." I answered, "But if you send me to school, my friends will find out and I told them that I was going to war." He just smiled at me and said, "You are going to school and since you have enlisted, you have to obey." He killed my spirit. That wasn't my plan but God had other plans for me.

When he saw that I got angry he said that after I get my G.E.D., he would re-consider sending me to Korea and that I had a good spirit because I wanted to fight for my country. He thought I wanted to fight but I just wanted to see the world and have a good time. He said that I needed time to grow up first so I was off to school. It took nine months for me to get my G.E.D. but first he gave me a 15 day furlough.

My mother thought I was going to Korea so when I got home with my duffel bag and in my uniform, everyone was expecting me to go to Korea so everyone was very sad. I was angry, I threw my cap on the floor and mom asked me, "Why are you angry?" I told her that it didn't matter at all that I had enlisted. I am not going to Korea! My mom jumped up all excited. She was so happy and everyone was hugging me. They called Pastor Manuel De La Cruz and everyone came over and they had a worship service at the house. My mom was singing along with the other sisters of the church who had been praying and fasting for me not to go to war. Mom told me that an evangelist had told her two weeks ago that she did not have to worry about her son because her petition before heaven had been answered.

The church had many men who were drafted and had been killed already so people were really worried about me enlisting. When mom told me about that, I got even madder. I left the house before the Pastor got there. I enlisted and then my family and these church people were praying against what I wanted the most, boy was I angry! God had answered their prayers. I stayed away for three days. At night I would go the military base and stay in the barracks by myself. I was too angry to go home. When my furlough was over, I went back to school. I could go home on weekends but I did not, I stayed in the barracks. My parents would come and take me home sometimes.

I had a graduation ceremony and I received a diploma. I would stay in the barracks anxiously waiting for my orders. Even though the war had ended, many didn't know it was over and some said the war continued in caves. Nobody came with my orders so I went to the Commanding Officer's office with my diploma in hand to show him. You just do not go knock on your Commanding Officer's door without an appointment or being called there but I did. I knocked and he said, "Come in." He liked my salute. I walked in and showed him my paperwork on the school graduation. He told me he was proud of me because I had obeyed his orders. I told him I wanted him to know that I was ready for Korea. He started to laugh and told me that the war was over and that the fighting had stopped. The United States had signed a treaty with them. Then he said, "Let me congratulate you." He got up from his chair and walked around his desk and extended his hand to me. We shook hands. He then said that he had another school in El Paso, Texas that he wanted me to attend and that it was for top secret training. They had done my security clearance while I was in school at Lackland.

I was transferred to El Paso. The C.O. told me that the Military Police Training would be harder than the basic training. I was there for three months. We had camouflage, biking, marches with field packs and went on long hikes. When I finished military police training, I was sent to top secret training where I was taught about airplane operations, how the airplanes are sabotaged due to Korean and Chinese terrorists breaking in and blowing up the airplanes. The school trained us to inspect the B-52 and B-36 planes. Korea was afraid of these bomber planes because they could fly very low or very high and were able to drop bombs from these heights. When the training was over, I was told that I was not going to Korea so I march right up to my Commanding Officer in El Paso and explained to him that the C.O. in San Antonio had told me that I was going to Korea after this training. He said, "I am your C.O. now, no one else and we are not sending anyone to Korea, we are withdrawing men from Korea." I got even angrier. I told him I would request a transfer.

From the military police in El Paso, I was transferred to Durant, Oklahoma and I went right into the motor pool so I could drive a truck. At Durant, after they had seen my papers, the Sergeant asked me, "What are you doing here? You had a very good job in El Paso. You were in the military police, that is a clean job and you get to wear good looking uniforms, here you are going to wear fatigues." I didn't care, I was happy there. I stayed in the motor pool for about two and a half years. Even though I was happy there, I still wanted more. I was never truly happy. I had other ideas.

CHAPTER TEN

The Ravens

> *"And it will be that you shall drink from the brook **and I have commanded the ravens to feed you there.** So he (Elijah) went and did according to the word of the Lord, for he went and stayed by the Brook Cherith, which flows into the Jordan. **The ravens brought him bread and meat in the morning and bread and meat in the evening and he drank from the brook."*** 1 Kings 17:4-6

JUST BEFORE WE RECEIVED THE BUS; God had given me a dream. I had been praying and asking Him if we were in the right place. People were asking me why I did not have a church or a decent house and why we were living like hippies. I would often talk to God about that and one night I fell asleep and dreamt about Elijah and how God sent ravens to feed him by the brook. Everybody was dying of thirst and hunger at that time but Elijah had plenty of water to drink and he was being fed daily by ravens.

One day, my wife and I and a few others were praying under a tree and we heard people behind us walking toward us. It was a Mother Superior with a few nuns walking next to her. Someone in the neighborhood had told them that there was a family living under a tree and that they needed help so they came to see what they could do. The Mother Superior, in those days, wore a habit, a large black covering over her entire head that extended to both sides and it looked somewhat like the wings of a bird. When I saw her, I knew that it was the raven God had sent to us. Sister Dolores was one of the nuns that came with her that day.

They were so gracious and asked if they could provide some food and things for us. We spoke for a while and I ended up giving them my testimony. When they heard my testimony, Sister Dolores cried and so did some of the other nuns. God had touched them deeply through the work He had done on my life. I asked them if they knew Jesus and if He was in their heart as Savior. They could not answer me. I asked them if they wanted to know Him as their Savior. They said they did so they knelt down and they accepted Jesus Christ as their Lord and Savior. Some said they knew Jesus but I told them that they only knew Him historically but not as their Savior. I told them religion cannot change anyone but Jesus does. When Sister Dolores got up from praying the prayer of salvation, she pulled out a fifty-dollar bill from underneath her black robe and gave it to me. She saw that we did not have anything to eat. She said that I would see her again very soon. As she was leaving, she said, "If I bring you people, will you tell them what you just told us?" I said, "Yes!" She then said, "And if I take you places, will you tell others what God has done for you?" I said, "Yes, I would be glad to do that." The next morning, she returned and she had several bags of food with her. She said, "I did not bring you any meat because I see that you do not have a refrigerator but I will bring you a refrigerator soon." I told her that I did not have any electricity and she asked me what else I needed. I then told her that we had no running water, no sewer, no gas nor electricity. She said, "We will have to work on that, won't we?"

She left and then the following day she brought Father Patrick Flores to visit us. He was not the Bishop of San Antonio at that time but she wanted me to tell him my testimony so I did. Many other priests and nuns would come by and everyone wanted to hear my testimony. I was glad to tell them and introduce them to Jesus as their Savior. I would witness to them and tell them that I wanted to help drug addicts. On one such day, Sister Dolores was there for a visit and she gave me a bag of money. She said that they had picked up an offering for us and she handed it to me. The bag felt heavy and I could not wait to count it. In those days, every dollar was so important to us. As soon as she left, I counted it and it was three hundred and sixty dollars. We were so happy. I took my wife to McDonald's and we ate hamburgers and French fries. We did not have a stove so we took extra to take home to the kids and the other drug addicts that had begun coming around wanting to hear more about Jesus.

One of those addicts that had decided to accept Jesus as his Savior and break the habit of drugs was Pancho Terrazas, Juan Terrazas's brother. He was a really good cook so he would cook for us all. One evening, for dinner, he dug a hole in the ground and then he wrapped a whole chicken with potatoes, carrots and onions in a clean burlap sack and then put a piece of tin over it and covered it with dirt. He buried the entire thing and then built a fire on top of it. The chicken cooked slowly for several hours and when we ate it, we were all surprised to find that it was the best tasting and juiciest chicken any of us had ever eaten.

Within three days of Sister Dolores' last visit, she returned and informed me that they had filled out the application with the City to get electricity to Spaatz Street. She also told me that water was also being provided to our street by the City and that all the fees had already been paid for. It would have been very expensive for us to apply for it, but God provided for everything. Even the temporary meter, the pipes and the faucets, all were completely paid for. In the span of just one month, we received a bus, electricity, running water and even a water cooler for the bus which provided cooled air for us during those hot Texas days.

Later Sister Dolores provided a refrigerator for us, just like she said she would. We could not put it inside the bus since things were already so tight so we built a little shed for it. Afterwards, Sister Dolores began to take me many places so that I could give my testimony. I would speak against drugs and always give a salvation message. Many received Christ as their Savior. She would take me to churches, groups and individuals in small towns in the surrounding areas. She also took me to the Lady of Guadalupe Church, Bonaventure Church, San Juan de Los Lagos Church and St. Mary's University. One day she took me to a large office belonging to a Priest off of Loop 410 and San Pedro and I testified to him as well.

About a year had gone by and we still did not have a restroom so one day, Sister Dolores asked me why we didn't have a restroom. We had been using a portable outhouse. Every two weeks the company would come by to clean it out. I told her that we did not have any sewers. She immediately said that the City needed to add sewers to that side of town. She worked for the Alamo Area Council of Government so she said that she would inquire about sewers.

At the end of a year, we were still living on the bus. Joel had not found a buyer for it and we had about fifteen (15) men living with us by then. We did not have any regular income coming in. The men were not working since they were breaking the habit but Sister Dolores was always faithful and gave us a weekly offering. She helped us for almost fifteen (15) years doing things for us that would have taken so much longer and so much more money for us to accomplish. God sent her to us to accelerate the provision and the establishment of the ministry He had called me to do in San Antonio, Texas. She was the first of many ravens that God sent to feed and provide for us.

One Sunday late afternoon, after the first year, she came over to visit with us. It was her day off but she loved coming by and sitting with us. She lived behind St. Vincent de Paul Church. She asked me if I had ever read the story of Elijah and I told her yes. She said, "Did you know that the ravens fed him?" I replied that I did and she said, "Every time I read that story, I feel like a raven myself." We all laughed because everyone there knew that I secretly called her "my raven". I then told her about the dream and she said, "I know it is God who is always placing you in my heart." She asked me, "Do you believe in the Virgin Mary?" I told her that I did, that I believed she was the mother of the Savior and that if it were not for her that we could not be saved. It was God's plan for Mary to be chosen to give birth to the Savior. She asked, "Do you believe in the heart of Jesus?" I said, yes, Jesus is inside of me. She asked, "Do you believe in the saints?" I replied, "Yes, I do and I told her the names of some of the saints in the Bible, the Apostles and the Disciples. I explained to her what a saint is, which is someone who is separated from the world to serve God. Someone committed to serving God with all his heart, soul, mind, and strength, which is the greatest commandment (Matthew 22:37-38). I mentioned some of Paul's epistles and how they mention the saints in Rome, the saints in Colosse and Corinth. I read some passages to her and she said, "I have read those passages before but now I see them differently."

During the time that Sister Dolores worked with us, we were flat broke; we had nothing but faith in God. We used to have Bible Studies under a tree and we would all congregate and she would come to listen to us. She liked to hear the testimonies and she would cry. She had a very sensitive heart and so much love to give. She learned to sing our worship songs and she would get into "la onda" with us; singing "coritos" (songs) and dancing to the Lord with all of us. She loved to hug everyone when she danced before the Lord. She would give everyone a holy kiss and tell us that this was "real religion", to help others and rejoice in the Lord together.

I never saw this kind of genuine love in the church that I grew up in. But I saw it in this Catholic nun, Sister Dolores, who loved and supported us and the vision that God had given me with all her heart, time, talent and treasures.

After one task was completed, such as getting electricity or water, she would ask me with enthusiasm in her voice, "OK, what's next?" One day she asked me that and I replied, "Sister, we are going to have to build a house." So she would say, "Alright, let's see what we can do, let's start praying." I started praying for the means to build a house. I was not a carpenter and I did not have any building tools; but God already knew all of that.

One Sunday afternoon, I was reading the paper and I noticed an article stating that the City of San Antonio was selling houses at a highly reduced rate if they were moved after purchase. They had purchased the land around Frio Street and they wanted to move the houses that were on that property. I went to talk to the City Manager. I explained why I needed a house and we started talking and I began testifying to him. He gave me seventeen houses and I was to tear them down and haul them off. They were for sale originally but he gave them to me free of charge. That night I told my wife and all the men living with us and we all rejoiced in that blessing. Then we began praying for a carpenter so he could show us how to rebuild the houses. We started tearing the houses down around Frio Street. We had to buy the tools to tear them down. We did not have a way to haul the wood but in the meantime, we began tearing them down and cleaning the wood of all the nails. The third day that we were out there, someone I knew drove by, saw me and stopped. We started talking and I gave him my testimony. He was so surprised to hear that I had given my life to Jesus and that I was working with drug addicts to change their lives. He asked me how I was going to haul the wood away since I did not have a truck. I told him, "I am not sure yet, but I know God will provide." So he tells me that he wants to give me a truck to help me. It was a 1956 pickup truck with six cylinders. I told him that I did not have any money and he tells me that he wants to give it to me. He was a plumber so this truck had pipe racks so we were able to carry the wood easily. We hauled a couple of loads that day.

The people in the neighborhood saw us bringing all this wood, windows and other items to our property and they wanted some of the wood or a window for their own house. We ended up giving the wood away so we were not advancing much because we were giving everything away. We helped the elderly put windows into their houses and repaired porches, rails and walls. We would even haul it straight to their house when we saw that they needed it so badly. When we started pulling the plumbing, some of the ladies would see the tubs and we would end up giving everything away.

We did not bring one single door or window to our land. Every time we had a door, window, tub, faucets or sinks, we would find ten ladies desperately needing help. I did not feel right saying no to them but at the same time, we needed a house ourselves. The guys from the rehab program would tell me not to give it all away but my heart could not tell them no. So the men started chasing the neighbors off when I was not there. We had a little problem arising there. In the meantime, we were still praying for a carpenter and we still needed to be taught how to rebuild a house.

At the end of a long hard day of tearing houses down, my wife would tell me, "You work all day, Sonny, and you don't bring anything home for us to build a house." I would tell her of the great need in the neighborhood and where every item went. She would then say, "Sonny, we must come first and then the men in the program. Make the house first and then afterwards, what is left over you can give away."

On night, in the middle of the night, around 3am, I woke up and walked outside. I was walking around the bus and talking to God. I was giving thanks to Him for everything and especially my salvation. I told Him how happy I was to know Him and how thankful I was that He had changed my life. I heard Him tell me, "Go to a lumber yard and go get the lumber you need to build your house." He told me to figure out everything I would need and to tell them. The problem was that I did not know what I needed because I was not a carpenter. So I thought about it and I knew I did not have any credit and I did not know how to figure out what I needed but Guadalupe Lumber Company kept coming to my mind. I told my wife that God was telling me to go to Guadalupe Lumber and she laughed. She said, "What makes you think you are going to get credit to buy lumber, you do not even have a job or any money."

The next day I went to Guadalupe Lumber and asked who I should talk to about getting some credit and they told me I had to speak to the owner, Phil Caruthers. I went to his office and told him what I needed. I told him that I wanted to build a three-bedroom house, living room, one bathroom and a kitchen.

He asked me if I had the building plans. I told him that I did not. He showed me some plans he had in his office and said that he would give me those plans if I bought the lumber from him. The plans were worth about five hundred dollars. I asked him if he could figure out what I needed and he assured me that he could. He immediately went to work and figured out everything that was needed. The lumber, shingles, plumbing, nails, insulation, pipes, everything I needed and how much I needed to build that house according to his plans. He totaled it up and it came to six thousand seven hundred dollars ($6,700). He said, "All you need now is someone to put it together for you." Then he said, "How do you want to pay for this?" All I had was one dollar and fifty cents ($1.50) in my pocket; I did not even have any gas money. He gave me a credit application and said to fill it out with all the information. All I put on the application was my name and address. I did not have any references. Any references I may have had were all negative. I had no credit whatsoever. My father used to say that no one would even give me a bag of scorpions on credit.

In just a few seconds, I handed back the application to him. I signed it and that was it. He asked, "What about the rest of it? What about your work history?" Mr. Caruthers asked me, "Don't you have any credit?" I replied, "I used to but I lost it all because I used to be a drug addict. He asked, "Are you still a drug addict?" I said, "No, I have given my life to Jesus and now I don't steal or use drugs anymore but I need someone to take a chance on me. I do not know how I am going to pay you back but I can assure you that I will pay you back every cent." He asked, "Do you have someone that will co-sign for you?" I said, "No, and I would not even dare ask anyone because I have burned so many people in the past. Then he asked, "Who told you to come to me, who recommended you to me?" I said, "I will tell you the truth, last night I was praying while walking around the bus where we are living right now. I have some guys that have come to me for help and they are living with us and breaking the habit of drug addictions. As I was praying, I felt someone tell me to go to Guadalupe Lumber; it came to my mind instantly. Currently, the guys and

I are knocking down some houses that the City gave us. We are tearing them down but every time I haul the lumber and other things from a house to my property, people from our neighborhood request it and I end up giving it to them because they need it so badly. We are not getting anywhere because I keep giving everything away." He stopped me and asked, "Which houses are you tearing down?" I told him that they were the ones on Frio Street. He then said, "We placed a bid on those houses, we wanted to buy them from the City and we were going to sell the lumber to Mexico but we were told that they had been given away to a rehabilitation center just getting started. So it was you that got those houses?"

He smiled and then extended his hand and shook it and said to me, "I am sorry but we do not give credit to anyone who is not employed. If you could promise me to pay so much per month, maybe I would think it over." I said to him, "Look, I need the lumber and all the material really bad but I would be lying to you if I promised to pay you so much per month. Right now, I cannot do that." He replied, "How are you going to support all those guys living in the home?" I answered, "I believe that God will support me and all the men He brings me just like I believe that He will provide all the things I need to build a house."

He looked at me intensely for a few seconds, picked up the application from his desk and dropped it in the trash can. He then handed me the plans for the house and gave me the list of supplies he had just made for me. He said, take these plans to the back and give them to a man named Lalo. He will give you all that you need. I shook his hand again, thanked him and walked out of his office.

Lalo was a deacon at Brother Morgan's church and he had been trying to get his boss, Phil Caruthers, to donate some lumber to his church for quite a while now. He was a little upset when I handed him the list and told him that Mr. Caruthers had authorized me to receive these supplies. Lalo immediately noticed that there was no invoice attached. He looked at me sternly and asked, "Do you have a way to haul the lumber?" I said, "No, he said to tell you to deliver it for us." Lalo could not believe what he was hearing.

As I was leaving, my uncle Josue Sanchez was walking into Guadalupe Lumber. He was a very good carpenter and he built houses for Mr. Caruthers. He gave me a big hug in front of Phil Caruthers and Phil said to me, "Do you know this man?" Josue answered immediately, "Yes, he's my nephew." Then Phil turned to my uncle and said, "You know Josue, I did something I have never done before in my life. This man has never worked a regular job in his life but I am taking a chance on him and giving him credit of $6,700." Josue said, "He is my nephew but he has always been the black sheep of the family but God has done a miracle in his life. Did he come to ask you for credit, Phil? Because before God changed his life, he would have come and stuck a gun in your face. But God has truly changed him and I know he will not fail you." My uncle hugged me again, really tight and said, "God is going to bless you, Sonny, you see how he has already touched Phil's heart to help you." My uncle then asked Phil, "Did he tell you how he is going to repay you?" Phil said, "He did not say, only that he would pay back every cent." Josue said, "You know what? I am going to take part in this ministry and I will pay the first $1,000. Put that on my account, Phil, I will take care of that." That same day we had the lumber and all the supplies delivered to our lot and our first one-thousand-dollar payment was made.

As my uncle was walking me to my car, he asked me if I needed anything else. He said he had heard that we were living like hippies but that he had mentioned my name and the miracles God had done in my life everywhere he went. He had found out that my testimony was well known in all the churches. So I told him, "We now have the lumber and supplies, Tio [uncle], but I need a carpenter, I don't know how to build a house." He said, "Look, right now I have a lot of work but I am going to get you the right man. I will get you someone who will get the building permits as well."

My uncle contacted Pastor Jerry Juarez and the presbytery of the Assemblies of God, the Southside Section and Pastor Oscar

Guajardo of Luz Apostolica Assembly of God Church. They were good carpenters and had already built churches and many houses. So now we had the lumber and supplies and the carpenters but now I needed a way to pay for their labor.

About a week later Pastor Jerry Juarez dropped by and said that my uncle had asked him to come by and help me build a house. He asked if I was a carpenter and I replied that I was not. He said, "Your uncle asked me to help you but I see now that I will have to do it all myself." I said, "I am not a carpenter but if you tell me what to do, I know I can help and I have several other men here that can help as well. We will do what you tell us to do." He then said, "Ok, I will not build the house for you but I will show you how to do it. Every day I will guide you and you will do it all. I will teach you how to build a house and you will be able to build more houses; deal?" I was happy with the deal until he said, "Ok, now let's talk business." I thought to myself, "I thought we had just talked business." He said, "The best part of the business is the money, now how are you going to pay me? Who is going to pay me, you or your uncle?" I said to him, "I will pay you and since you don't know me, if you want a contract, we can write something up." He said, "I am going to charge you by the hour, even though I am not going to physically do the work, I am charging you for the training, the gas, the food. I will probably be here three to four hours per day and I will charge you $10 per hour so you will pay me $40 per day, are you ok with that?" I agreed to that.

Then he said to me, "How are you going to get the money? I don't want to work for two weeks and then you tell me that you are getting the money by faith. I do not work by faith; I work for money." I knew that he had been working with my uncle and with Guadalupe Lumber for over twenty years building houses so he was used to having something steady and secure. I said to him, "Look at that lumber over there, brand new lumber, do you know where it came from?" He said, "Yes, your uncle told me that God did a miracle with Phil and that he gave you credit when you did not qualify for it." I said, "That's right but you know Phil and you know that he does not give anything away to anyone. So who actually gave me that lumber, Geraldo? His eyebrow rose up and he started to think and after a few seconds he said, "God gave it to you." I said, "That's right and just like God gave me that lumber, He will also give me the money to pay you." He stared at me for a while and then gave me his hand and we shook on it. He said, "We don't need a contract, we can start tomorrow, four hours at ten dollars per hour, which is forty dollars per day."

The men sitting around were listening and they were praying while Pastor Juarez and I were talking. They were tattooed men with no shirts on; some had the Virgin Mary on their backs and the devil on their arms. They came over to us to thank Pastor Juarez for his help. They were happy that they were going to have a house. Then they began to pray for him and some begin to speak in other tongues, thanking God for His blessings and rebuking all hindrances. The Pastor never closed his eyes; they were wide open with amazement. When the prayer was over, Pastor Juarez said that the scripture, "Watch and pray" came to his mind during the prayer.

He came back the next day, very early in the morning and he brought Pastor Oscar Guajardo with him. We now had two carpenters and they began squaring off the land. They showed me how to square off the lot and then the house. They marked about 30 holes that needed to be dug to place the house foundation on. The men and I had to dig down about 24 inches deep and 10 inches in diameter for each hole marked. He left me a stick and measuring apparatus to go by. After four hours, Jerry and Oscar left and the men and I worked very hard, long after the sun had set, until we could not see anything. Jerry left me digging tools and a flat bar. We did not use shovels; we used our hands to dig. In the morning, he could not believe that the holes were ready and exactly like he wanted them. The width and depth was perfect. We worked long and hard because we were desperate for a house.

When the lumber had been delivered, the men used the bundles of wood as beds. They were grateful, every night they would take a bath behind the bus with a water hose and in the morning, we washed and brushed our teeth using cans and bowls.

Jerry and Oscar were in total shock to see that all thirty holes had been completed perfectly. They then told us that they usually take a full week to complete that work. We had not started digging until after 12noon but had worked late into the night. When they arrived the following day, they found us praying, walking between the holes, thanking God for giving us the strength to finish and the blessing of the house. When I saw Oscar and Jerry that morning, the presence of God was already among us and they could feel it too, Pastor Jerry was moved to tears.

That second day, Jerry showed me how to insert and level the post into each hole. He showed me how to level it, how to measure it and put a rod right in the center of it. That was all he did that day. We needed gravel, sand and cement. After he left, we started working and worked until about 10:30pm. In the morning of the third day, they returned and could not believe we had done a three-day job in one day. They always arrived when we were praying in the morning. We were just finishing our prayer time when one of the men asked Jerry if he was a minister and if he would give them a Bible Study. Jerry said, "I came to build a house, but I can give you a Bible Study, sure." He went to his truck to get his Bible. This was the beginning of our Bible Studies before we started to work each day. Pastor Jerry gave us really strong studies in the word of God, it was solid teaching. After our Bible Study that day, we began working with the beams. Jerry showed us how to do one beam and then he left. We needed fifteen beams in all. He cut it, nailed it and showed me how to cut them and nail them and set them on top of the posts. We did not have a hammer or an electric saw. He lent me a hammer and his hand saw. But I promised him that with the next offering I received I would buy myself a hammer and an electric saw.

That is how Pastor Jerry (Geraldo) Juarez showed us how to build a house. Within two weeks, we had the skeleton of the house set up and all we had left was to cover it. The men started to sleep inside in two weeks. In the meantime, we had not paid Pastor Jerry anything yet. He had been writing down his hours and the first week I had to initial it to confirm his hours. We were now in the middle of the second week, I figured I owed him about four hundred dollars. I did not have four hundred pennies on me. One Saturday, he called me and said, "I have to pay some bills so I am coming over to pick up my paycheck." I did not have it but we had been praying for it and we knew we had to pay it so I told him to come over.

I told the men what we owed him and that somehow we had to pay it. I reminded them that it had to be clean money and so we all prayed in earnest. We knew God would take care of this. So when the men knew that Pastor Jerry was on his way to pick up the four hundred dollars and we did not have it, one of the men said, "Go and hide and we will tell him that you are not here." They all had some ideas on how to get the money but none of them were right. Pastor Jerry only lived about ten minutes away so we needed a miracle right away. We needed $400 right now! Some of the men were praying in tongues, some were crying and then Pastor Jerry drove up. I told the men, stay inside and keep praying because if I tell Pastor Geraldo we do not have the money, he may not come back and we need him really bad. Lydia was there also and she was praying as well. Lydia suggested that I give him our car or go get a loan out on the car or call Sister Dolores. None of the ideas I heard were from God.

Pastor Jerry asked me, "Have you had breakfast yet? Get in the car; I am taking you to breakfast." I did not know what to do, I did not even have money to pay for my breakfast; I was getting a little nervous. I was not going to hide from him so I had already washed up and changed my clothes. He started driving and said, "I am going to take you to get a good steak." He drove to Cattlemen's Grill on Frio City Road. That was an expensive restaurant; now I was getting really nervous. We sat down and he ordered for both of us. While we were eating, every time he started to say something I was sure he was going to ask me for the money. When we finished eating, I put my hand in my pocket like I was going to pay for my meal but he immediately said, "No need, I am going to pay for this." We left the restaurant and were standing in the parking lot when he took his time card out and said, "Look it has been ten days, do you know how much you owe me?" I said, "Yes. I do not have it on me but let's go back to my place and I will get it for you." So we got into the car and I said, "Go to the left" but he turned to the right. I said "You're going the wrong direction; the money is to the left" but he just kept going. Then he gave me his time card and said, "You know what, here's my time card, you can rip it up or throw it out, it doesn't matter, you do not owe me anything." I said, "But I want you to come back. I do not want you to think that I am not going to pay you." He said, "Don't worry about that, I am going to keep coming back. You just do not know what God has done in my life since I have been working with you. I have learned so much from you about faith. I am a teacher of faith but I have never seen faith like I've seen in you and the men you serve. I know now that you can actually see faith with your own eyes because I am seeing it every day in you. I am going to help you, Sonny, and I am going to keep coming but now I am going to work eight hours instead of just four and I am going to give you my hammer and I am going to lend you my electric saw." We had already cut hundreds of 2x4s to be used in the walls. We had cut 62 2x6s to make the trusses and we had cut another 62 2x6s for the ceiling joists. He had never seen anybody saw that much wood with a hand saw. In one day, we had cut all of those pieces. God spoke to Pastor Geraldo and showed him faith through us. He never asked for any money after that and he continued coming until the house was finished. Pastor Guajardo came with him too and he never asked to be paid. Pastor Guajardo would pick up offerings in his church for us. After a month, we pretty much had most of the house done. About that time, Tio Josue came by to see how we were doing. His sons owned a drywall company named A-1 Drywall so he called one of his sons to see if they could help with the drywall. We needed electricity so my Tio Josue found us an electrician. They came and put the electricity in and his sons did all the sheetrock that was needed. Our Heavenly Father provided all that we needed and paid for it himself.

Every time I would take some money to Phil Caruthers to pay

my bill at Guadalupe Lumber, he would never take it; instead he would give me an offering. Although I tried many times, I never did pay that bill at Guadalupe Lumber. In the end, he said, "You do not owe me anything." While we were building, Phil would come to see us and bring men with him so that I could give them my testimony and lead them to Jesus. He became a partner in our ministry so he would come by to see how the house was coming along. Many times I would see him drive by and point to our house.

Another raven that was sent by God to feed and provide for us was Serapio Rodriguez. I have never known a man more sensitive to the Holy Spirit than this godly brother. He was a plumber by trade and it seemed that every time I prayed to God for a specific need, Brother Lapo, as everyone affectionately called him, would show up and get the job done. He never asked for payment and when I tried to pay him he would say with a smile, "I've already been paid." He brought toilets, sinks, faucets and all the plumbing supplies and items we needed for our home, dorms and kitchen. I never had to call him, the Holy Spirit would send him and he always seemed to show up exactly when he was needed. I thank God for that man of god who blessed us with innumerable things at just the exact time when we needed them the most. Brother Lapo was my brother-in-law's father. My brother-in-law, Joe, is married to my sister Frances and I grew to love and learn from that Christian family so much. When Brother Lapo passed away, many were at his funeral that stood up to say what a blessing he had been in their lives. How this man had given and given so much and never asked for anything in return. That man expressed the love of God through his generosity and willing heart.

My brother-in-law, Joe H. Rodriguez, is also a man of high integrity and generosity. He is the one that helped me set up my non-profit organization when I initially returned from California and he served as a Board Director and President of San Antonio for Christ for well over 30 years. He was a co-founder, along with me and my wife. He is now retired but he was a seasoned businessman and without his help, it would have taken me much longer to get organized and structured properly. His help was invaluable. Joe is a godly man who does everything in excellence and I was blessed to have his experience and wisdom guiding me on my Board. He helped with the incorporation of the non-profit, the accounting and all the legal and reporting requirements. I had no experience whatsoever in that area but God provided someone who He could trust completely to walk hand in hand with me for over thirty years. He also provided and installed the acoustical ceiling tile that we needed for our buildings. He is a man of faith and a prayer warrior that is faithful in all that he does.

Without these godly-sent ravens, and many more that came, I could not have done what God asked me to do. They fed us, supplied all our needs, opened doors to us, provided all that we needed and never asked for payment in return. They just brought the blessings of God as we needed them and God blessed them in return in inexplicable and obvious ways.

CHAPTER ELEVEN

The Miracles

> So Jesus said to them, "Because of your unbelief for assuredly, **I say to you if you have faith as a mustard seed,** you will say to this mountain, move from here to there and it will move and nothing will be impossible for you." Matthew 17:20

Genaro's Miracle

GENARO HAD BEEN DISCHARGED FROM THE ARMY because of his severe injuries. He told us that since he had left the army hospital, he had been in constant pain and the pain killers were no longer working for him. He started seeking out "curanderos" (witch doctors) for relief. He had been to the Texas Rio Grande Valley and Mexico looking for them. The curanderos would give him various remedies for the pain but none of them worked. One of the witch doctor's remedy was for him to jump the fence to get to a neighbor's chicken coup and steal some of the eggs exactly at midnight. He could not borrow the eggs, he could not walk around the fence, the instructions were explicit. He was to bring them back to his house and put the eggs on his neck where the pain was. Of course, that remedy did not work at all. He kept going to different curanderos but he never received a cure or relief from his pain and every remedy they asked him to do was illegal. He was going through his savings fast and had nothing but frustration and pain to show for it. The last curandero was near Monterrey, Mexico. He was told to get the toenail from a lion. Genaro could barely walk much less run from a lion. They were just taking his money and giving him false hope. When he came to us we were having a Bible Study. He sat right in the middle of our living room and he patiently waited for me to give him some kind of task to do; a secret remedy that would heal him. Just before the bible study was dismissed, Minister Javier Martinez walked in and started singing a "corito" called "Solo Dios hace al Hombre Feliz." Genaro was sitting in his wheel chair and then all of a sudden he jumped up from the wheel chair and did a summersault in front of everyone and landed standing straight up in front of all of us. He started telling us right away that he felt a human hand on his neck and around his belt during the song and when he felt that hand, his pain was completely gone. Genaro and his wife could not understand the supernatural power of God to heal and they became afraid and left right away but not before he accepted the Lord as his Savior.

We kept having our Bible Studies and Genaro and his wife, Susanna, came to the next one. Genaro said that the minute he walked into our living room he felt that same hand on him and he never felt pain again from that very first time. That day, Susanna received Jesus Christ as her Lord and Savior as soon as we finished singing "I'm so glad Jesus Set Me Free."

My Wife's Family is Miraculously Transformed

Lydia had been praying for her family's salvation and particularly for her brother, Mencho. He had said to us that he would rather go to hell than become a "holy roller" like us. The day of his miracle, we had called Mencho to build a porch for us at the house and Lydia started witnessing to him. He told us that he was not going to do the work because we could not afford to pay his high fees so he left. Our Bible Study started later in the evening and just a few minutes after we started, Mencho's car speeds up to our house and he runs into the house barefooted and yelling that his daughter, Janie, was dead. Lydia walked out to see him and asked him where Janie was. She was in his car so she went out there to see her. Janie was paralyzed with her eyes opened but she was not speaking or moving. Thankfully, she was still breathing, very shallow, but still breathing on her own. They brought her into the house but I kept on with the bible study. I ignored Mencho since he had said that he would rather go to hell than be like us but in my mind, I knew God was working on him. I felt God telling me to go on with the study. Mencho was at the door with his eyes wide open, he saw that I was not stopping the bible study so he ran to the pulpit and yelled out to God, "Help Me! I am sorry for what I said, please help my daughter." God humbled him. He was crying like a baby so I went over to minister to him. I lifted him up and asked him what had happened to Janie. He said that he was at home lying down and resting when he heard Janie and her mother yelling and fighting in the next room. They were in the kitchen and then Janie slapped her mother. Her mother cursed her and then Janie froze and fell back stiff and paralyzed; like she was dead. God quicken my spirit and told me that a demon had entered her because she opened the door to her soul when she hit her mother in anger and disrespect. When I started ministering to her, I whispered into Janie's ear to ask God for forgiveness for hitting her mother. Mencho told me that she could not hear me that she was paralyzed and could not speak. I kept whispering into Janie's ear to ask for forgiveness with her mind and to tell God that she would never hit her mother again. Janie did not speak but she started to move her eyes. I knew she understood me.

Then she started speaking but it was not her voice. It was the voice of a man and it said, "Janie is mine." I started talking to the demon and telling him that Janie belongs to Jesus and to get out of her. When we rebuked the demon, Janie began crying and asking God for forgiveness in her own natural voice. When she did that, Mencho and Janie both fell on their knees and began to ask God for forgiveness and both received Christ as their Lord and Savior. I then asked my wife to get her mother, Licha, to come over right away. We had to minister to the whole family. Licha also asked God for forgiveness and accepted Jesus as her Savior. The whole family got saved that night.

Licha had an appointment for surgery that week and she said that while we were praying for her, she felt a hot hand inside her stomach in the area that was bothering her. She did not know anything about God or His healing power so she did not know what was actually happening to her. It was God showing His intense love for her and healing her. She was astonished by the whole experience, especially when we told her that she was healed. After that, others in the group felt the strong presence and power of God but they were not sure what it was. Others received their healing that night also and began telling us what they experienced. It was like a spiritual battlefield that night in our living room and God was getting all the victories. Unusual healings, salvation and deliverances from generational curses were seen that night.

The Seed of Building a Church

That night people started talking about starting a church and having me as their Pastor. I never wanted to start a church; I just wanted to have a rehabilitation home. I knew we needed a church but I did not want to sing in front of everyone. I always noticed that the Pastor would lead in singing. All these thoughts were going through my mind that night as people kept talking about starting a church. Then they began to tithe, pulling money out of their pockets to get started that same night.

We had to buy land to build a church and next to our house, there was vacant land but we had no money to make a purchase. I knew the owner of the land and I was aware that the lots were being sold for eighteen hundred dollars ($1,800). The very next day we all met for prayer and to discuss our plans. We came to the decision that we should buy a lot in payments and agreed that I should go talk to Mr. Shafer, the landowner. After everyone had left, I went over to visit with Mr. Shafer. I went to his office and I talked to him about the property. He had a map and I showed

The Miracles

him the lot we wanted, which was right next to the house. He quickly said, "I can build a house for you." I said, "I want to build a church." I asked him for the price and he gave me the price of $1,800. I told him that I wanted just one lot. He said, "I can give it to you on payments but you need a down payment first." I did not have a down payment for him. He then said, "Why buy just one lot; I have twelve lots on that side all the way to the end of the street. Why don't you buy all twelve? I also have another twenty lots on the other side of the street." I said, "No, I just want one lot." He then asked, "What kind of church are you going to build?" I replied, "I don't know what kind of church." He asked, "What kind of preacher are you? Are you a self-made preacher?" This opened the door for me to give him my testimony and tell him about my past and how God called me into the ministry. I also told him that God had sent me to Bible School in California and then sent me back to San Antonio and that I was just getting started in the ministry. He asked, "What about the house, is it yours?" I told him how God had provided miraculously for us through Guadalupe Lumber Company and how He had sent us carpenters and all the trades we needed to finish it.

He replied by saying with a smile, "Are you giving me a hint so that I will give you the land, what are you trying to do?" I said, "Oh, no, I did not come to ask you for anything but I am only telling you the truth. I don't work a regular 9 to 5 job like most people but God always provides. I believe God will help us just like He did with our house." Then Mr. Shafer said, "I am going to do something for you. I am asking $1,800 for each lot but I am going to give them to you for only $1,000 each; which will only be $12,000 for all twelve lots." I said, "That's just too much, I can buy one now and then later buy another one, one by one." He said, "What happens if you buy one today and then later someone else buys another one, what will happen to your church?" I jokingly replied that I would take down all his signs so that no one else would be aware that the lots were for sale. We laughed and then he said, "I am going to make you a deal that you can't resist. He said, "Look, you can give me twenty dollars down and twenty dollars per month with no interest at all. I will give you the property deed on them and keep a lien on the lots until they are paid off. What do you say?" I said, "I can't because twenty dollars on each lot is two hundred and forty dollars a month and we cannot afford that." Mr. Shafer said, "You are not listening to me. You are going to pay the twenty dollars down for all twelve lots and then twenty dollars per month for all twelve. When you can't pay the twenty per month, come to me and I will give you the twenty dollars." So we agreed and I left his office with a whole bunch of papers, all the deeds to all twelve lots. I was singing and praying in tongues all the way home and we rejoiced that night.

There was a lot of work to be done because that meant more clearing of the lots, twelve lots, dealing with snakes, rats, possums and skunks. When I got home, Sister Dolores was there. I had already told Lydia about our blessing of twelve lots. I called her from Mr. Shafer's office. They were all singing and dancing and rejoicing when I drove up. Sister Dolores came up to me and gave me a big hug and a kiss on the cheek. She said, "I knew something was happening in the spiritual realm because I have been praying all night and I knew Sonny was up to something. I did not know what it was but I knew you needed some help, so I prayed for you." She was so excited; she was jumping up and down, dancing and praising God for the huge blessing He had just given us.

As I walked her to her car, she said to me, "I want to make the first payment." I thought she meant the first twenty dollars but she meant the first payment for a lot. She wanted to pay the whole amount for the first lot so she gave me one thousand dollars before she drove away.

The next day I drove to Mr. Shafer's office and gave him the first one-thousand-dollar payment. He was shocked and amazed and shook my hand with enthusiasm.

God Continues to Provide and Heals my Son

My brother, Andrew, started to come around and at that time, his wife, Mary was very ill. They would come and we would pray for them. One of those times, after our prayer, I told them the story of Sister Dolores giving us one thousand dollars to pay for our first lot and Mary said excitedly, "I have felt for a long time now to give you two thousand dollars and now that you are telling me that story, God has reminded me again. Andres and I have been arguing about it but this time we are going to do it." That night they gave me a check for two thousand dollars. The next day, I went over to Mr. Shafer's office and when he saw me coming, he jokingly said, "Do you have another one thousand dollars for me?" I said, "No, I have two thousand dollars!" Again, he was shocked and amazed and smiled at me with disbelief.

Back at the home, we were all rejoicing because of all the blessings and the miracles and how God was providing for us so miraculously. We had the titles to all the lots and we started blessing the land and claiming that ground for the Lord. We cried tears of joy. Suddenly we realized that we had someone ill in our house. Sammy, our son, was just one and a half years old and when he was born, the Doctor told us that he had an illness that affected his kidneys and that his lungs had holes in them. The Doctors showed us his x-rays where you could plainly see the holes in his lungs. Each lung had a hole in it the size of a nickel. When Sammy was only six months old, we had to take him back to the hospital because he could not sleep. He cried all night, he was not growing properly. His stomach was overly bloated and he had a very bad odor especially when he urinated. The Doctors told Lydia that the only solution was that they should operate but that Sammy was not strong enough for the operation. They sent Sammy home and said that if he survived for another six months that they would reassess Sammy to see if he was strong enough to have surgery. They told us that Sammy could not live much longer without the operation. So we brought him back home and kept him for eight months but he cried most of the time, ate and slept very little and did not grow much.

We were rejoicing over all the blessings of the land, our faith was high and then Lydia told me that the hospital had called asking us to take Sammy for a reassessment for surgery and that if he was strong enough, they would do the surgery immediately.

Just then it seemed like the devil was on a mission to steal our joy. In the morning, Lydia took Sammy to the hospital. We all prayed in agreement that they would not have to do the operation and that Sammy would be healed completely. Not long after my wife left, she called to tell us that they had admitted Sammy into the hospital, he was in a room and they were prepping him for the operation. I told Lydia that I was on my way to her. I was mad and upset. When I arrived I went to see Sammy right away and he was crying non-stop. He did not want anyone to touch him. Lydia asked me what I was going to do. I said, "I am taking Sammy home!" I went to the nurses' station and told them that I was going to take my son home. The nurse said, "No, you can't take him, we just admitted him, he needs an operation." I replied, "I am taking him home." She called the hospital security and the doctor. When I picked him up from his bed, the doctor walked in. He was upset with me and he said, "Your son is very sick, Mr. Perales, and I am going to operate on him in the morning. If you take him, he is going to die and if he dies, you will be placed in jail." I said, "He is not going to die, I am taking him home and we are praying for his total healing." The nurses and the security and several doctors were all there now and they told me, "You could pray for him here at the hospital." They followed me all the way out of the hospital. I could hear one of them saying behind me that I was a religious freak and fanatic and that God would punish me and the law would charge me with murder. When I got in the car, a Police cruiser pulled up next to me. We were already in the car and the policeman came up to my window. The policeman said, "Give me your son, Sir." I said, "No, I am not going to give him to you, Officer, this is my son and you cannot take him away from me." He said, "Your son belongs to the State, now give him to me." I replied angrily, "No, he does not belong to the State, my wife had him and he belongs to us." I had my driver's side window about halfway down, the engine was running and the doors were locked. The policeman reached in and tried to grab the keys but I had the car in reverse and I stepped on the gas.

I said to him, "You'd better get out of the way." He pulled his hand out of the car and I rolled the window all the way up. As I drove away, he was yelling at me that he would get a warrant and put me in jail. I sped off, got on Interstate Highway 35 and came straight home from the Santa Rosa Hospital. I did not even see what Lydia was doing all this time, I assumed she was getting in her car as well and driving home. As I was driving with my son, God was giving me scriptures and saying, "Everything I give you is good." God and I were having a serious conversation and I asked Him, "If You did not give me Sammy then take him, Lord, but if You gave him to us, then make him right. You are not a man that You should lie and You said everything you give me is good; make Sammy good." I was crying out to God and driving home at 70 miles per hour.

When I got home, my wife was already there and she was hysterical; she thought that the police had arrested me. I had previously told her that if the doctors operated on Sammy that he would never be right again. I drove up, got out of the car with my son and placed him in his playpen. I took her by the hand, called all the men from the house and said, "Look, we are going to pray but not all at the same time. We are going to do what the bible states to do; pray with understanding. We are going to pray in complete agreement for our son. I do not want anyone praying in tongues, pray with your understanding. We are going to talk to God and put Him to the test and see if He is for real." The men were all looking at me with fear in their faces but I was completely serious with God and with them. I grabbed the Bible and started looking for the scriptures that God had given me as I was driving home.

The first scripture was; "So you shall rejoice in every good thing which the Lord your God has given you and your house, you and the Levite and the stranger who is among you." Deuteronomy 26:11

The second scripture was; "God is not a man that He should lie, nor a son of man that He should repent. Has He not said and will He not do? Or has He spoken and will He not make it good?" Numbers 23:19

I explained the meaning of those scriptures to the men and my wife and then I said, "This son of mine is not right but God only gives good things so I will pray and you all will stand in agreement with me, got it?" They all agreed.

I started praying and saying, "God you gave me this son and if your word states that everything you give is good and that you are not a man that lies then make this son of mine right and if not, then take him right now. I want You to take him right now if you did not give him to us but if you did, then heal him and make him whole." While I was praying and my wife and the men were agreeing with me, Sammy stopped crying and began to fall asleep in his playpen. He had not slept much at all, just very short intervals, so he must have been very tired so we let him sleep as he lay in his playpen. We continued to pray. It was 3pm when we started to pray and Sammy fell asleep and at 6pm, he was still sleeping. He slept for three hours straight and that had not happened in a very long time. He did not cry when he woke up, he just sat up in his playpen. Sammy had never stood up before but this day, he stood up and we were all amazed to see how calm, peaceful and happy Sammy was and that he was standing on his own two feet. That was a miracle in itself. He usually did not like for people to touch or pick him up but on that day, Neche, one of the guys, picked him up and he was smiling and happy. He brought him over to the dining room where everyone was having dinner and immediately all could see the difference in Sammy and they started thanking God and rejoicing for the healing and total transformation in our son. We all noticed right away that the awful odor that Sammy used to have was also completely gone. It was not there anymore and he was not crying at all. His total disposition was different and we claimed his healing with great praise and faith that day. Who knows what kind of continuous pain my son had been in but that day it was all gone. Neche took him to sleep in his room that night and from that day on, they were inseparable. Neche loved to call Sammy "cowboy."

The following day, early in the morning, three nurses and a detective arrived at our home and demanded to take Sammy. The men of the home were determined to fight for Sammy; they were not going to allow them to take him. Instead, we all started to witness to them and they saw the difference in Sammy themselves, so as it turned out, they did not take him. We ended up leading the three nurses and the detective to the Lord that morning. One of the nurses was very familiar with Sammy and she immediately saw the change in him. She was quickly convinced that something wonderful had happened. The Detective then spoke up and said, "I really don't want to take your son from you and from what the nurses are saying, maybe this really is a miracle and your son is healed but to be sure, why don't you take him to the hospital to get checked out that way we will know for sure and we can get this complaint against you settled. That would put you in the clear, Mr. Perales." I said, "All right, we can agree to that but please give us two weeks because I want Sammy to gain his strength and be able to walk by then." They all agreed to that.

In two weeks, we took Sammy to the hospital to be checked out thoroughly. When I called to make the appointment, the Doctor said to me, "If your son is still sick, I will take him away from you and do the operation he needs. I don't believe he is healed; there is no way that could have happened." I said, "My son is not sick and you will see for yourself tomorrow." My wife and I happily took our son to see that Doctor the next day. As we walked into his office, the first thing he said was, "Where is Sammy?" I said, "He is right here and I pointed to little Sammy who had walked in with us and was standing right next to me." The Doctor assumed that child was someone else, he expected us to be carrying a crying baby in our arms but that was not the case. Sammy was not crying and he was walking on his own. The Doctor had never seen Sammy walking. He had a look of shock on his face. He picked Sammy up, placed him on the table and started his examination. He asked me, "Are you willing to leave Sammy here with us?" I said, "Yes, I will but I am going to stay with him as well." The Doctor said, "That will be alright." I said, "Did you notice that Sammy is not crying?" He did not respond.

Then the Doctor pulled out Sammy's old x-rays and pointed

to the two nickel-size holes in his lungs and said, "The first thing I want to do is operate on his lungs." I replied by saying, "No, the first thing I want you to do is take another set of x-rays." They took Sammy for x-rays and when they were delivered to his office, the Doctor was astonished and could not believe that those x-rays were Sammy's. He insisted that they be redone. The nurse took Sammy again to be x-rayed. When the second pair came back identical to the first pair, he was now indignant and accused the nurse of not doing it right and said that he was going to take the x-rays himself. When he saw the third pair of x-rays, he then said, I don't know what kind of trick you are trying to pull here, Mr. Perales, but this is not the same boy." They had Sammy's footprints and handprints on record so the Doctor took his footprints and handprints again to compare them and said to me, "I don't know what you are trying to pull but I am going to catch you. I am going to get an expert to match these prints for me and when I find out that you are trying to pull something over me, I will personally go to your house and take your son away from you." I said to him, "You don't believe that this is Sammy?" The Doctor said, "Yes, I believe that this is Sammy but I know that something is wrong somewhere and I am going to find it." I replied by saying, "There is nothing wrong anymore, Doctor, there used to be something wrong with Sammy but God fixed all that and now everything is right with my son." He got even more upset with me when I said that. He could not accept that reality. We left his office and came home with Sammy.

Two weeks went by and they did not call me so I went to see the Doctor. When I walked in, he asked, "Is Sammy sick?" I said, "No, not at all, everything is perfect." So he asked, "So why are you here?" I asked him, "Did the prints match?" He said, "Yes, they did." I then asked him to check Sammy's kidneys and his reply was, "Well, if God healed his lungs, then He must have healed his kidneys also." I said, "That's exactly what I wanted to hear you say, Doctor." He gave me a half smile and then said, "Bring Sammy back in two months and we will do a thorough examination and if his symptoms act up before then bring him in right away." He also said that in his entire medical career he had never seen anyone healed from what Sammy had suffered so just to be on the safe side, he wanted to send a nurse to check on him once a week. I agreed to that. The nurse was to come every Monday for three months. She arrived the first Monday and she received Christ as her Lord and Savior. She came for only a month and she reported to the Doctor that Sammy was truly healed and in perfect health and there was no need for her to keep checking on him. A few months later we called the Doctor to see if we had to bring Sammy in and he said we did not have to bring him in any longer, that his case was closed and that it was marked as a "healing" from God. He and some of the nurses that worked with Sammy were dealing with patients that had advanced cancer and they began calling us for prayer for their patients. We gladly prayed for them each time a request was made and even though we never heard back from them, we were confident that God was healing in beautiful and unexpected ways.

CHAPTER TWELVE

The Miracles Keep Coming

> *"For with God, **nothing will be impossible.**"* Luke 1:37

God Releases More Amazing Resources

DURING THIS TIME, SISTER DOLORES WAS WATCHING all the miracles and her own faith was soaring. She would bring people by and we would testify to them and talk about the miracles God was doing. The people she brought were nuns and priests. One day she wanted us to take Sammy to Father Patrick Flores' office; she wanted him to see the miracle God had performed on Sammy. Sister Dolores was the main one to encourage us to start a church. We had all the property we would need now, three of the lots had already been completely paid for and now Sister Dolores wanted to pay for the fourth lot. Most of the lots still needed clearing so one day a Suburban from the Air Force drove up and Sister Dolores got off with five military officers. We were in the middle of our Bible Study when they drove up and came in. We took a break to introduce ourselves and greet them. She said, "I brought these men to you so you can tell them your testimony. I started telling them about my past and how God had healed me, my son and all the men there. When I finished my testimony, some of the Officers had tears in their eyes and they all ended up accepting Jesus Christ as their Lord and Savior. After the prayer, she said, "I brought these men here to hear your testimony but also so they can help you. Tell them what you need." I showed them the land where we wanted to build a church and how it was full of brush and trash, people had been using it as a dump and it needed some serious clearing and cleaning.

The very next day, they brought dump trucks and heavy equipment and begin clearing the lots for us. They cleaned everything all the way to the end of the street for us. They did all the heavy work in less than a week because they had the right equipment and they brought plenty of men.

Sister Dolores was insisting that we build a church and I was still very hesitant so one day she told me, "I am going to pray to God that He show you exactly what to do with that land, not what YOU want to do with it but what GOD wants you to do with it." Then she asked me, "How do you want God to show you? What sign do you want?" I said, "I need all the material to build a church, I need everything!" She confidently said, "I will pray that God show you what to do."

The next morning during our morning prayer time, the phone rang in Lydia's room and she came in and said, "You are wanted on the phone." I was upset because of the interruption during our prayer time and I was not going to take it but she said, "The man said it was very important." I went to the phone and it was a Lieutenant from one of the Military bases. He asked me how we liked the work that was done for us by the men in the Air Force and I told him that we were very grateful and that they had done an excellent job. He asked, "Are you going to build a Church?" I replied, "I am not sure yet." He then said, "I think you should definitely build a church and we leveled the area right next to your house really good since we thought that would be the perfect place for your church." I thanked him and then he said, "Those lots are all cleaned up, do they belong to you?" I said, "Yes, but we still owe on them so I am concerned that if we build a Church and then something happens where we can't purchase the lots, we would lose the church." He said, "How many lots do you need to build that church?" I said that I thought we needed four lots but then we would also need a parking lot. He then asked, "If the lots were paid for, would you build a Church then?" I said, "I guess I would but I don't have the money to build or to pay for the lots right now." He replied, "What if I help you pay for the four lots?" I said, "I would build a Church then." The Lieutenant said, "Maybe I can help you pay for the lots, I know you don't have the money and I don't know why I am getting into this, I don't even go to Church myself but I know this Church will be different. I'll see what I can do. I couldn't sleep last night; I kept having all these plans and thoughts in my head that's why I called you so early this morning. Thanks for taking my call, I will be in touch." We hung up and God released a peace and confidence in me that I had not felt in a while. I knew then that God wanted me to build a Church and that He would provide all that we would need.

God Removes All the Debt and Sends More Help

I went and told them what was going on and the men were so excited, they wanted a Church for sure. The next day, the Lieutenant called again and he said that he was working on something and that I would hear from him pretty soon. He said, "I have some Army barracks that you could tear down and use for material to build that Church." I said, "I can't until I pay for that land." He quickly responded by saying, "Don't worry about the land, I am going to take care of that for you." The next day he came to take us to go look at the barracks that he was considering giving us and he even said that he was going to give us fifty men to help us take them apart. The very next day we started taking the barracks apart. The Air Force also offered us use of their heavy equipment and tools to get the job done and to transport the wood. It was during the summer and it was over 100 degrees outside. I was working with 40-50 men and the day was grueling. When I got home, my wife told me that Bernabe Lugo had called and he wanted me to come over right away. I was totally exhausted and I did not want to go see Bernabe. He was a drunk in those days and had so many problems. My wife said to me, "You want to save men and when God calls you to minister, you are too tired?" She put on a Christian record, a 45 rpm, which my brother Joel had just recorded. It was a song called, "Without Him". She called Bernabe to come over to our house instead. The song was playing when he and his wife walked in. All of a sudden, Bernabe got on his knees. God touched him and saved him that evening. We prayed for his wife and she also gave her heart to the Lord. That was the first husband and wife that got saved under our ministry that were not drug addicts. I was still very hesitant and nervous about singing in front of everyone as a Pastor but Bernabe was a good singer and he was also a carpenter. After we prayed for him, we started to talk and I shared with him our plans for a Church and right away, Bernabe volunteered to build the church for us. Bernabe was Genaro's brother so he had already heard about the miracles God was doing in our ministry. He and his wife started attending the services and bible studies and he started working for the Lord right away. He started building our Church. The people from Lackland paid off the four lots so we started building on that land. After we finished tearing down the barracks, it was enough to frame the church. We still needed to finish it and we did not have shingles, sheetrock, floor tile, paneling or the electrical that would be needed. As it turned out, Genaro was an electrician so he did all the electricity for the church. They gave me a list of all the things we needed and I went back to Guadalupe Lumber Company to talk to Phil. I told him that I did not want him to give me anything; all I wanted was for him to extend some credit. The amount we figured that was needed to finish was three thousand nine hundred dollars ($3,900).

He did, he gave it to me, he said, "I am not going to give you credit, Sonny, I am going to give it to you." So we finished the church but we did not have any pews. Sister Dolores came by for a visit and she noticed that we needed pews. She went to talk to Archbishop Furry. He obtained the pews for us from a Catholic Church in Seguin who was remodeling their church. They were very good pews and they even rented a truck for us to transport the pews to our Church. God built the Church for us. He sent the people with the skills and equipment to do it, sent the labor, the funds to pay for the lots and all the finish out material from Guadalupe Lumber Company at no cost to us. He even sent us some great looking pews and a good singer to lead the Church services in song and praises. God provided all that we needed and exactly when we needed it.

Expansion, Acceleration and Preparation

After the church was finished, Sister Dolores said, "Now you need a mess hall; a church is not a church without a mess hall." So we all started to pray that God would provide a mess hall for us. About that time, Sister Esther Gallagher started attending our Church and she said, "I was raised in a Baptist Church and I know how to do fundraisers." She wanted to sell dinner plates and she set a goal of selling one thousand plates. We made the tickets to sell them at two dollars and fifty cents ($2.50) each. But before we started selling those tickets, we were faced with a greater need of higher priority. Several men from the home who had been saved and had been delivered from drug addictions were hungry and eager to go to Bible College. Mingo Berlanga, Eddie Vera and Joe Gonzales were insistent on going to Bible College. I went to go talk to Brother David Coote, who was the Director of International Bible College. I had a hard time with Brother Coote because he had never had drug addicts in his college and he wasn't sure how the other students and the parents would react to that. This was something new to him. I started to witness to him and tell him how I had graduated from Latin American Bible College in La Puente, California. I told him how God had called me to build a rehab home and a church and how God was preparing the men for ministry so going to Bible College was very important to them. He asked me, "Do these drug addicts bathe, cut their hair and dress properly?" I told him that they look just like me and then I began to give him a rundown of our ministry and the miracles God was doing through us. I said, "Many people don't understand it but it is definitely God's work and the miracles speak for themselves." He said, "I have never seen a drug addict attend Bible College so I will have to speak to the Board and get back to you." He had never heard of David Wilkerson, Nicky Cruz or Sonny Argonnzoni at that time.

Later that week, he called me and said that he had met with his Board of Directors and that they had decided to accept the men as students at the Bible College but there would be rules to be followed specifically for them. The rules were that we would have to pay the full amount up front for each student. They could not live in the dorms and their meals would not be included; they would have to bring their own lunch every day and they could not use the dining room. The men could not stay on campus after classes; they would have to be picked up right away. The cost would not include any field trips. We agreed to all their rules. The school tuition was twenty-seven dollars and fifty cents ($27.50) per year and it was a three-year College. So now we needed to raise the money to send these men to Bible College so I spoke to Sister Gallagher to sell the plates but instead of the funding the mess hall, the funds would be used to send the men to school. I felt an urgency to send them to Bible College because I did not want them to turn back to their old ways; I wanted them to get a solid foundation in Bible College as I had done. Sister Gallagher was on board and she sold 100 tickets the first week. Then later, ten people sold one thousand tickets. We made lots of food, sausage, potato salad and beans. I took care of the beans myself. We were all busy cooking inside the house and outside. It was August and it was extremely hot that summer. In the middle of all this work, I was told that someone was looking for me. It was a white lady. I had never seen this young woman before; she was about 21 years old. Her name was Ann Bennett. She said, "You probably do not remember me but I came to one of your services here recently. Last night, I could not sleep and God told me to come to talk to you and give you a check for your ministry." She handed me a check. I took the check and without looking at it, I put it in my wallet and thanked her. She said, "Look at the check, please". I took the check out of my wallet and looked at it quickly and my first thought was that it was for $250.00 but when I looked at it more carefully, I saw that it was for $2,750.00. She asked, "Is that the amount you were asking from God?"

She then said, "God told me to tell you something, I hope you won't get offended at this but He told me to tell you that He called you to preach not to run a restaurant. He said to tell you not to sell food but to give it away. He said that He can give you more money than you can make selling food and that if you don't listen to Him and keep selling food, you will never prosper. You are supposed to give it away."

She continued and said that last night she could not sleep and that God had given her a vision of our ministry in the future. She said I saw your street, all the way down to the dead-end; you are going to have a lot of buildings. In the buildings, I saw the rooms full of food, stacked up high. I saw a lot of people lined up to get food. God told me that people would be coming here from far away to get food. I saw many rooms and they were all packed with food. God said to tell you that if you obeyed, all that would happen. He also said that if you continue to sell instead of giving the food away, He will let you do that but He will not bless you abundantly the way He wants to bless you. I told her, "I will obey; I know it is God talking to me."

I got in my car when she left about 2pm and I drove off; leaving everyone still cooking and preparing plates. I went to pray under a bridge along Loop 410. I repented and told God that I was new to this ministry and how He does things and that I did not know that selling food was wrong. I prayed and cried to God that afternoon. I stayed there until about 10pm. I had been gone for many hours and no one knew why I had left or where I was. The next day was Sunday and many were mad at me because I had left in the middle of all the work that had to be done. They had good intentions and good hearts but they were offended. I showed them the check for $2,750.00 and told them the message from God that Ann Bennett delivered to me. Some started to murmur because their plans for fundraising were now upset. I told them that from now on we were going to make food but we were going to give it away. Sister Gallagher said, "Pastor, you don't know what you are going to lose."

We eventually sent seventeen (17) ex-drug addicts to Bible College and before the first semester ended, Brother Coote called me and said, "We have three hundred students here and I wish all of them were like the men you sent." He said that the men were an example in everything; in how they dressed, how they spoke, their conduct and in their prayer and worship life. He also said, "Next year send all the men you want and if you don't have the money up front to pay for them, don't worry, we will take payments." I used to drive them myself every day and although the classes started at 8am, we would arrive there at 6:30am and would go straight to the chapel to pray. The men brought their own lunch every day and for the first few months, they were not allowed to eat in the dining room but that changed very quickly after Brother Coote saw their conduct and great hunger for the word of God. They began to cut the grass at the College free of charge and pretty soon, Brother Coote took them everywhere he went.

The check we received from Sister Bennett we used for Bible College for the men and the plates brought in $2,500.00. We got everything we needed and we never sold any more food. God supplies all our needs once we are obedient to what He wants us to do. Through the Texas Vocation Training organization, God provided twenty-five (25) scholarships to a four-year Bible College including books and an income for each student of about $400 per month while they studied. We could pick the major so we chose "Christian Theology" at Isleta Assembly of God Bible College in El Paso, Texas. We had just started the Church, we had about seventy-five (75) members at that time and many of them left because they did not agree with me about not selling plates. In their opinion fundraising was a good way to raise money and they wanted to do that instead of trusting God for the provisions needed.

As for me, I know that God desires obedience over sacrifice all the time so obeying God is my first priority. Trusting Him to provide is my "greatest rest and joy" in His promises.

No Signs of Life – Yet Alive!

In 2011, I, Pastor Sonny Perales, was in my home and the next minute I blacked out and woke up in the hospital six days later, completely paralyzed. I could not recall what happened, could not remember how I got there and did not remember receiving any visitors and speaking with them. My wife and children had to fill in the sequence of my events moment by moment.

My wife, Lydia and my daughter, Elizabeth, were with me when I blacked out and they drove me to the hospital. When I was examined in the Emergency Room I had no signs of life whatsoever. They rolled me in to take quick x-rays of me and they showed that my intestines were twisted and they had burst and were bleeding contaminants into my blood stream. My intestines appeared totally black in the x-rays. Two Doctors examined me and my wife was told that they would not admit me because I had no signs of life and that I would be taken to the morgue instead for a full autopsy. As my wife and daughter disputed with one of the Doctors, another Doctor saw one of my fingers move but still they were not convinced that there was life in me. My daughter asked for a second opinion and when there was a delay, they decided to take me to another hospital. My wife and daughter were praying constantly that God would intervene with mercy and healing.

Upon arriving to the second hospital, another set of x-rays was taken immediately and these x-rays showed no twisting, broken or bleeding intestines and neither were they black; the intestines were now white. I was admitted into the hospital right away and placed into intensive care. For six days my life hung in the balance. My family was told that I might not make it another 24 hours. My children, brothers and sisters were notified to visit me right away because I may not survive the night.

During the next six days the Doctors told my wife and family to make funeral arrangements and if I survived a week that I should be placed in Hospice. They were told that I would never walk again and that I may never regain consciousness. On the sixth day, I woke up but did not remember how I got there. Family and friends began to visit me in the hospital, I did not recognize any of them but I spoke to them as if I knew exactly what was happening in their personal lives and I gave them advice and direction. While in the hospital, a few days later, my throat closed completely. I could only speak in shallow whispers. My voice was barely audible. I could not eat or drink anything. A feeding tube was placed in me so that I could take in nutrients. I lost twenty pounds in that first month. After that first week in the hospital, the admitting nurse came up to see me in Intensive Care; she could not believe I was still alive. She told my family that it was a miracle indeed.

I was released one month later and brought home to recover. My mind was still very fuzzy, people would tell me things that had happened or things I said but they did not make any sense to me, I had no recollection of any of it. I did not even realize I was back in my own home until days later. My feet felt like cement. I could not move them. I was still paralyzed. My son, Michael, would take me to church in a wheelchair and they would pray for me and each time I was prayed for, I felt my legs gaining strength. After a month or so, I now felt I could move my feet again and I began trying to lift my legs. I was given a walker to try and begin walking but I was still very weak and could hardly hold myself up. I was still on the feeding tube and could hardly talk at this point.

I was having severe hallucinations and nightmares almost every night. I could not get a good night's sleep and my wife stated that I was kicking, punching and jerking in bed all night long almost as if I was fighting with something or someone. She had to sleep in another bed because I would accidently hit her during my nightmares. My mind was filled with flashbacks from my military days; experiences that I had tried to suppress for many years. Overwhelming feelings of sadness, heartbreak and depression were surrounding me, I felt a darkness coming into my mind and my life like I had not experienced in all my time as a Christian and a Church Pastor. Before I gave my life to Jesus Christ, I was a drug addict so I had certainly experienced darkness and evil in my life but had not felt it since surrendering to Christ. Now my mind was filled with what "appeared to be the truth" but it was deception, lies and wickedness. I felt that I could not pray anymore, I was convinced that God did not love me and that He was not going to hear my prayers. My mind accepted the lie that God had not forgiven me for my sins and that He had walked away from me. I did not feel His presence. I felt no emotions at all, just cold distance from Him. All those thoughts appeared to be the truth in my own mind and I could not break loose of those dark and deceptive thoughts.

One day my sister, Frances, her husband, Joe and their daughter, Lili, came to pray for me. Lili sat close by listening to the small whispers I was saying to her parents about my nightmares and how I believed that God had walked away from me and was not going to hear my prayers. My wife and sister both kept telling me that God loves me and that He would never walked away from me but I was convinced that I was right and they were wrong. They were not going to change my mind with mere encouragement. After about half an hour of listening Lili came over and said, "Uncle Sonny, I understand that you believe this so let's say that you are right, maybe God is not hearing your prayers anymore but He will hear mine. Do you agree?" I said, "Yes, I know that He hears the prayers of His children but He is not listening to me anymore." She said, "Ok, but God also says that if two or three come together in His name, there He will be, right?" I said, "Yes, I believe that." Lili said, "Alright, then I want you to repeat the words I say, will you do that?" I thought for a long time and then I said, "But God is not listening to me, nothing will happen." She said confidently, "But God is listening to ME and I KNOW that He hears my prayers and there are more than two here that are in agreement for your total healing. All you have to do is repeat my words, will you do that?" She was looking straight into my eyes; she didn't flinch a bit. There was a long silent pause where no one said anything; everyone was waiting for me to reply.

I finally said, "yes" in a weak, whispered tone and nodded with my head. She said, "Ok, let's begin; remember to repeat every word I say." She began praying a prayer of thanksgiving and praise and then asked for forgiveness for sins and to receive healing and miraculous restoration of mind, body and soul. I repeated every word without hesitation but did not really believe the words I was saying. I felt no emotions at all; I did not feel the Holy Spirit during or after that prayer. I thought nothing had happened; there was no emotion on my face at all and I felt no different when the prayer was over. But then she said, "I am going to pray for your deliverance now and that is going to put things in order so that you can receive your healing." She began praying and I closed my eyes. She first welcomed the Holy Spirit into the room and immediately I felt the presence of God. Something lifted off of me that very moment and the power of God moved through my body and mind. Everyone in that room felt the divine presence of God sweeping through them. I felt a hot wave going through me and tears started streaming down my face uncontrollably. I had not felt that way in a long while. I knew we were in the very presence of God. She began calling out ungodly spirits like the spirit of fear, infirmities, depression, unforgiveness, unbelief and confusion and with authority she told them to leave. She set a supernatural boundary of protection around me, my family, my ministry and my property with the precious blood of Jesus. She called on godly spirits such as faith, love, joy, peace and grace and asked them to occupy my mind and heart. She commanded 100% healing and restoration to my mind, body and soul and everyone was praying in agreement with her. From that very moment, when I heard those words, my mind began to clear up. I felt my mind turned that day. Confusion began to leave, lies and deception were removed and only the solid truth of God and His Word flooded my mind. The truth of God's promises and His holy scriptures began to fill my thoughts and memories. That day I began my journey toward total restoration and healing. Today my mind is clear and strong. My memories are all back. I can walk on my own, speak perfectly and even drive my own car again. I sleep soundly. I have not had any more nightmares or flashbacks. I have been healed and restored completely by the power of the living God, Jesus Christ, whom I serve with all my heart, mind, strength and soul.

Even when there are no signs of life, God is the god of ALL life and He is on your side. When it looks impossible, remember that nothing is too difficult for Him. Do not let your faith falter. Do not believe a Doctor's report of death, disease or negativity when Jesus Christ is The GREAT Physician and it is His loving will that we be healthy, strong and miraculously healed. Trust in the God of unconditional love and receive your miracle. I was told I would not survive the night but years later, I am still here enjoying the blessings of Jesus Christ, His unconditional love and my family and friends.

Pastor Sonny Perales
San Antonio For Christ Church
San Antonio, Texas

CHAPTER THIRTEEN

The Bus Ministry

> *I was naked and you clothed Me;*
> *I was sick and you visited Me;*
> ***I was in prison and you came to Me."*** Matthew 25:36

IT SEEMED LIKE WE WERE GETTING BLESSED with gifts from God and yet the people were not happy, they wanted to raise the money and not let God provide. When God provides, He gets all the honor and all the glory. The people wanted the glory; they wanted the pat on the shoulder for a job well done. I was being obedient to God because He had given me the message that if I wanted to sell plates, He would have given me a restaurant. Some church members sometimes just do not understand the Pastor. Many had come from other churches where fundraising, by selling food, was very common.

Sister Gallagher was the one who always wanted to help me. She had a very good heart and she always wanted to help me raise money but I had to do what God wanted. The drug addicts' mentally is for the woman to support them. I only wanted to obey God; afterwards Sister Gallagher learned to give and understood what I was talking about. At that time, Sister Gallagher had a son in the penitentiary and she did not know where he was exactly.

She wanted to go see him and had even decided to walk, if she had to. She knew he was in Huntsville somewhere but didn't know which unit. There were six or seven units in Huntsville at that time. I felt sorry for her and told her that I would take her in my Toyota pickup. We went to Huntsville to the Walls Unit and as it turned out, we were blessed because that was exactly where he was. When we went inside, she spoke to the Chaplain and told him that her Pastor was with her and asked if I could minister to the prisoners. The Prison Chaplain arranged for me to be able to minister to the prison population.

We drove home and the next morning at church, Sister Gallagher gave her testimony. She told everybody about the things that had happened in Huntsville. Now Sister Zimmerle came and spoke with me after church and told me that she had her husband in the Ellis Unit and she also wanted a ride to visit him. The only problem was that I only had a Toyota and a standard at that. The Toyota pickup truck had the gearshift in the middle and a bench seat. So with three people riding on the seat, I decided I would train the Sister to shift gears for me so that I would not have to brush up against her leg while shifting gears. So the Sisters were happy to shift gears. The first time, I left Sister Gallagher at the Walls Unit and then drove to the Ellis Unit to drop off the other passenger. Then I would drive back to the Walls Units and pick up Sister Gallagher. When I drove up, Sister Gallagher was all excited.

She told me that she had a talk with Chaplain Pickett and that he wanted me to participate with the bible studies they had in the morning. We had to look for a motel so we could stay overnight so that I could be available first thing in the morning. This was a door that God was opening at the Walls Unit in Huntsville, Texas. We found an inexpensive motel and got two rooms, one for me and one for the Sisters. It was during the winter and it was freezing and it was about 4pm so we went to find something to eat. At night, about 10 pm, I wanted some coffee so I knew about Winchell's donuts in downtown Huntsville. I called the Sisters to see if they wanted to go with me but they said they were ready for bed but to bring back some for them. When I arrived at Winchell's donuts, it was real cold, almost icy. There were people outside on a bench, mostly elderly Mexican women. I went inside and got some donuts and when I came outside, I asked them if they needed any help. They weren't friendly at all but they said that they were waiting for the Greyhound Bus to come to take them to San Antonio but that it would be another hour before the bus arrived. I offered them my room if they wanted to warm up for a while. I told them I would bring them back before the bus arrived. They didn't want to, they were suspicious of me. I left a little sad because I couldn't help them. I told Sister Gallagher about what had happened with the ladies and she began to cry. She knew how it felt because she had not seen Bobby, her son, in five years. She felt sorry for the ladies. I also felt sad and I could imagine if it was my own mother sitting in the icy cold weather, waiting on a bus bench. I drank my coffee but I could not enjoy it because God was putting a burden in my heart. I started to pray and ask Him why the mothers have to suffer so much. I said, it's their children who have sinned, causing them to be in prison but it's the mothers who suffer silently. I asked God to help the mother's find a way to see their children. I thought about my own mother and how much I had caused her to suffer because of my own sins.

While I was all broken in the presence of God, He told me in an inaudible voice, "You help them." I thought right away, "How can I help them? I just have a Toyota. I don't have any money. What can I do?" I then heard an inner small voice saying, "Help them and I will help you." I couldn't even imagine how I could help; I didn't even know what I needed. I told God, "Yes, I will do it but I don't have any money."

The next morning, I got up real early because I had to bring the bible study. I prayed and got prepared for the Lord to use me. Both Sisters went with me and we made history because women were not allowed to go to the men's Chapel in those days but that was about to change that morning. On the way to the Chapel, I told them about my conversation with the Lord and they both started jumping up and down with excitement. They had been praying for God to talk to me and for Him to supply all my needs for a Bus Ministry. After the service, we visited the inmates in the Walls Unit. After we left there, we couldn't stop talking about the Bus Ministry. We decided we needed a van. We started praying on the way home for a van to transport people. Maybe we could trade in the Toyota truck for a van. Sister Gallagher knew people from the housing projects who needed to ride to the prisons to visit family members. We arrived back in San Antonio on Sunday night for the evening service. We walked in during the testimonies and Rosa Huerta was testifying and telling the congregation about her dream.

She saw a brand new yellow van parked in front of my house and I had told her that God had given it to me so that I could take families to visit the inmates. As she was testifying, the three of us walked in and we heard her dream. The next morning a Christian brother came to my house with a brand new yellow van. I had never met this brother before. He came inside and started telling us that he had just come out of the Calles Church t start his own church so he had purchased a brand new yellow van for his church but then his congregation had walked out. He asked me if I was interested in taking over the payments on this van. I asked him what he wanted as a down payment and he said, "I want nothing, just take over the payments and it's yours." He said that God had told him to come to my house and give it to me. This brother was working for the civil service and he had taken out a loan through his credit union and had signed a contract for the payments to be taken out of his pay the first year. He said, "I don't want any money at all, I have already paid a large down payment on this van and I will be paying monthly payments on it for the first year and if after the first year God wants me to continue paying for this van, I will. But if God doesn't tell me anything, then you take over payments." The insurance payment for the first year was also included. I agreed to take the van. As soon as he gave me the van, he gave me power of attorney and turned over the paperwork to me and title over to the church.

When I got the van, I drove over to Sister Gallagher's house

The Bus Ministry

to show it to her. I had to share this with her as she had been praying for this to happen. She was a prayer warrior. In less than one week, we had a list of people who needed transportation to the prisons to visit loved ones. We charged five dollars for the ride, just enough to cover the fuel. We had fifteen passengers our first trip. We were full on our very first trip. We met at Sister Gallagher's house at 2pm but we had a problem. When I arrived to pick them up there were 35 people waiting for me. There were so many people there that police squad cars and a fire engine truck was there also. What is going on!

From the moment I saw the need that the families of prisoners had to make a simple visit to their loved ones in prison, God placed a burden in my heart to help them. I prayed to God that He would bless them and make life easier for them but God's response to me was, "You help them." I could not see how it might be possible for me to do that but God made a way. He was just looking for a "willing and compassionate heart". Before I knew it, God has released a new Van and eventually a Bus to transport families to prisons all over Texas. A Prison Bus Ministry developed and for over ten years, I drove the bus and also lead many families and many prisoners to Christ. Below are two newspaper articles on this ministry. San Antonio For Christ and the various ministries that we did over the years were featured several times in the newspaper, local news and even on a global television show called The 700 Club.

Below are two newspaper articles that were published in the local newspaper called The San Antonio Light about the Prison Ministry that Sonny Perales started. The first article was published as a five-page featured story on July 8, 1984. The second article was published on July 21, 1986.

Our Father Who Art In PRISON

Every month, Sonny Perales helps reunite prisoners with their families. And thanks to Sonny, scores of inmates have found that God can touch the lives of the most hopeless and desperate men. Even behind bars.

By Sarah Pattee

It is 2 a.m. outside Mario's restaurant. A group of people stands waiting on the corner. The street lamps cast a stark white light over them. Mariachi music and laughter spill out everytime the restaurant door opens. The nearby freeway overpass rumbles with the weight of passing cars and trucks.

The night's energy doesn't touch the people. They stand silently, in eerie stillness in contrast with the revelry and noise around them.

Most are women, their arms full with babies, bags of diapers, and bottles and food in brown sacks. A few men stand off to the side, waiting silently, smoking cigarettes.

One little girl stands alone, clutching a toy red plastic suitcase. Half an hour earlier, her mother woke her up, dressed her in jeans and a sweater and bundled her off to join the group of waiting people. Inside her suitcase are a frilly pink dress, shiny patent leather shoes and a stuffed animal.

Her name is Diana Rodriguez, and she is going to visit her father in jail. Like the rest of this group, the 6-year-old is waiting for a battered, ex-Greyhound bus that will take her to a prison farm more than 300 miles away. There, for two hours she will visit her father, separated by a wall of steel-meshed glass, and surrounded by a room full of anxious relatives and inmates dressed all in white. The bus is driven by Sonny Perales, and if it weren't for him, Diana would never get to see her father, Reynaldo "Nayo" Rodriguez, arrested almost seven years ago for selling narcotics to an undercover cop. It was his third conviction. As a habitual offender, he was sent to jail for life while Diana was still in her mother's womb. For years after her parents divorced, Diana didn't see her father. Not until Reynaldo contacted the Rev. Sonny Perales, or Brother Sonny as he is called by the parishioners at San Antonio for Christ Ministries Church in southwest San Antonio. Every month, he leaves from his church, stops by Mario's, and then heads out to Huntsville. His two sons drive one bus and with a friend, Sonny drives the other. Together, they visit about 15 prison farms, traveling 700 miles, from 2 a.m. all day and into the next night.

For Sonny, this monthly trip to the Texas prison farms isn't just a journey; it is a personal crusade. The force behind this mission, he says, is the Lord. It was the Lord, he says, who pulled bleary-eyed, dope-addled Sonny Perales off the streets and made "me myself again." It was the Lord who stopped his wife from filing for divorce. And most important, it was the Lord who gave Sonny the push to help others, from his monthly prison bus runs to his weekly "testimonials" and chapel services he gives on his own at the prison farms. Who better to help, asks Sonny, than inmates sentenced to jail because of crimes committed to feed their drug addiction, those people who are shadowy reminders of what Sonny once was. Sonny is hooked on the Lord now and he wants drug addicts to know the Lord is a much kinder master to serve than heroin.

Diana's father Reynaldo is one of those whose life has been touched — turned around, really — by Sonny. An ex-addict like Sonny, today he can't string together a sentence without adding "Praise the Lord" or "God Bless You." He leads the choir and Sunday school at his prison. There is only one thing more important to him than getting out and helping other ex-addicts find the Lord. That is to be with Diana.

It is Diana and Reynaldo, and many others, who put Sonny behind the wheel of his big bus (also provided by the Lord) every month. For many of the inmates, this monthly, two-hour visit is the only time they see their families. For some, this is their only contact with the outside world.

Tonight the bus is a little late, and a few men dive into Mario's for coffee. When the two buses pull up, everyone pushes forward, eager to get a seat. Diana falls into the seat behind the driver and Sonny wraps a blanket around her. A jacket becomes her pillow. Soon, the only sound is the throaty hum of the bus as it heads out towards Houston, its headlights cracking the darkness. Sonny's sidekick, Arturo Garza, drives while Sonny talks about his prison buses, his life, Diana, the Lord.

For most of his passengers, including Diana, traveling with Sonny is the only way they could see imprisoned relatives. A round-trip ticket on a regular bus from San Antonio to Huntsville costs $55.60. A taxi from Huntsville to one of the outlying prison farms could cost up to $20. By offering a $20 round trip from San Antonio to any one of 15 prison farms, Sonny makes sure "old ladies aren't standing by the side of the road hitchhiking back from the prisons." And for those who can't scrape together even $20, the ride is free.

Not that the ride is first class. This bus is squeaky, and air whistles through the cracks in the windows. The seats and the floor are worn with 14 years of hard use. But no one minds, least of all Sonny. His prison buses are prized possessions and he loves nothing more than to roll up the sleeves of his neatly ironed shirt and reach into the engine in the back of the bus, his two sons not far behind. Sonny knows his buses inside out, from the sink in the bathroom to the exhaust system. His powder blue Cadillac, given to him by his devoted parishioners, doesn't rate as high as his buses. Even the abandoned, rusted-out 1948 bus behind his church is precious. That is where Sonny, his wife, Lydia, and two children lived after Sonny returned from Los Angeles to San Antonio in the early 1970s. At least, says Sonny, the bus was a step up from where they lived the first two months back in town — under a tree.

Born in San Antonio, Sonny, now 49, had fled to the West Coast when he was 33 years old, leaving behind his wife and two sons. He took with him a 15-year heroin habit he couldn't shake, despite time in the Fort Worth Penitentiary for selling drugs to a federal agent. Once in California, Sonny lived on the streets, begging money to buy drugs, wearing the same clothes for weeks. One day he stumbled into a rescue mission during a church service. There, he says, "I gave my life to the Lord."

Sonny's life spills out into the soft darkness inside the bus. The feeling is intimate, his voice soft among the sleeping people. Arturo is driving, and gospel music from his tape recorder fills the front of the bus. Sonny smiles a little as he searches for words to explain a life turned around in half an hour. He knows it sounds almost too simple, that change from hopeless junkie to hope-filled Christian.

"I didn't have anything left to lose. I had lost everything, my self-respect. That man who was testifying said he had been a drug addict. He knew I was going through withdrawal. He showed me his tracks from injecting so many years. How was it I could change, I asked him. 'Get down on your knees and ask the Lord to come into your heart.'" Sonny leans forward, his eyes burning. "He healed me right there. Since

CONTINUED

The Bus Ministry

CENTERPIECE

that night, the desire of heroin and alcohol and cigarettes have gone away." It wasn't a blinding flash of light or a voice from heaven that cured him, just something that happened. "I felt something in my insides. The withdrawal was gone. The hurt, the pain, everything was gone."

Sonny said he promised the Lord he would "dedicate my life to Him." He entered a drug rehabilitation program for four months and then enrolled in the Latin-American Bible Institute, connected with the Assembly of God church. There, in nearby La Puente, he studied the Bible and counseled drug addicts for the next four years. During that time he also called his wife in San Antonio to tell her of the great change in his life. At first she didn't believe him, and Sonny says she had plenty of reason not to. During their marriage, he had lied to her, stolen from her, beaten her and, "I had never told her I loved her in 15 years of marriage. When I said 'God bless you,' on the phone, she thought I was using drugs." But curious and hopeful, she came out to Los Angeles, three months after his conversion. Her first sight of him was at the airport where he was giving Bible tracts to a man. "I was laughing and talking and when I turned around she was crying. She had never seen me smile before." She decided his change was in earnest and moved out to Los Angeles with their two sons to be with Sonny.

Together, they returned to San Antonio; directed with a message from the Lord telling Sonny to return to his hometown and help drug addicts. Their first home was under the tree in the church yard, "where God wanted me."

Sonny is a strikingly handsome man. His hair looks like a dark stiff bush, combed back and spray-painted with white flecks. His face is smooth and serene and he looks like he has found his path in life. Following the Lord is hard work, and sometimes Sonny seems humorless. But every once in a while, his eyes grow warm and he smiles, especially when he is with children. (He and his wife now have four.) At one point in the ride, he cuddled Diana on his lap teasing her in both Spanish and English.

While he talks, the bus rolls through back country roads, north on State Highway 36, then State Highways 159 6, and then 30 toward Huntsville. Soon the sun is coming up, throwing a clear, early morning light over the damp, green fields of East Texas. Passengers are slowly coming awake, rummaging through paper sacks of food, drinking from thermos bottles. Not long after sunrise, the bus pulls into the first of the prison farms on the route today. Wallace Pack II named after Wallace Pack, a warden at Ellis Unit who was killed by an inmate. Most prison units are named after wardens, and a unit will bear the stamp of the man who runs it.

Wallace Pack I and II are the newest prisons in East Texas, and Sonny says they are more modern than the old, brick ark-like buildings of the main Huntsville Unit (called "the walls") because of the high walls surrounding the building) or Ellis Unit, where Diana's father is incarcerated. Instead of brick, Wallace Pack is a series of mustard-colored rows of buildings. Here inmates live dormitory-style with air conditioners and television. Instead of working in the fields, inmates are allowed to go to school and pursue a trade.

At the gate the guard a young fresh-faced man, peers in the bus and asks "Any firearms, drugs or liquor?" He then smiles sheepishly "I have to ask that." Arturo says in a low voice over his shoulder "You'd be surprised how many people say yes."

One of the two women stopping here is a weary-looking woman in her late 40s. She is going to visit her husband who, she says, "never had a record and they gave him 20 years." She adds bitterly "But it was self-defense." She gets off the bus and goes into a small outer building with a glass front. Because the prison doesn't open for an hour, she must wait in the tiny room. Then she must sign in with the guard, who will check her driver's license and make sure she is one of the 10 visitors inmates are allowed to see twice a month (up to two at a time). After a two-hour visit with her husband, she will wait seven hours before Sonny returns to pick her up.

For the next few hours the bus winds through the piney woods along small country roads, stopping to drop off passengers at the prison farms at Wynne, with its enormous chapel, or at the red brick buildings of Ferguson. At each stop, people get off and with a "hurry back" to Sonny, they head for the guard house. They are bare-headed, as visitors are not allowed to bring anything in for the inmates, although they can buy them soft drinks from the vending machines in the waiting room, give them to the guards who then give them to the prisoners.

During this time, Diana is waking up and Sonny gives her a pastry from a paper sack. She draws in her coloring book, stares out the window, teases Sonny and tries to get his attention. She is a shy girl with flashes of quick intelligence. If it affects her that her father is in prison, she doesn't show it.

Turning onto one of the many back roads around Huntsville, Arturo points out one building, the holding unit "There they cut your hair, give you shots. From there they tell you what farm you're going to go to, by your record. Wynne is for guys who can't really work hard, so instead of working in the fields they make license plates and furniture."

Arturo is the unofficial tour guide this trip, and he has first-hand knowledge of the "sights." Like Sonny, Arturo was a long-time heroin addict who spent a total of 10 years in Texas prisons As in the case of Reynaldo it was Sonny who led Arturo to the Lord Driving a bus every month seems to Arturo a small repayment for eternal salvation When he talks about his years in jail, Arturo switches from bitterness to hard-edged humor But whatever he talks about, he sprinkles "Hallelujah" and "Praise the Lord" throughout casually. A tall man with a wiry thin body (and prison tattoos that he

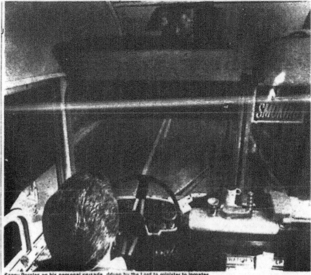

Sonny Perales on his personal crusade, driven by the Lord to minister to inmates

Sonny, center, holds Diana when the group stops for a lunch break

20/SAN ANTONIO LIGHT JULY 8 1984

keeps covered), Arturo's strongest features are his almost maniacal grin and bouncing energy. While talking, he picks out a cassette tape from the cluttered dashboard. The "hallelujah! hallelujah!" swells of evangelist Jimmy Swaggart fill the front of the bus, turned up louder now that it's daytime. Passing one prison farm, he looks around from his perch behind the wheel. "When I was there, do you know how much they gave me? $50. For two years, man... Don't spend it all in one place."

Arturo can still rattle off his prison number 2040608. "When you go in, they say, 'From now on, you're a number. Don't forget that number. It's going to be yours until you get out of here.'"

Sonny's prison bus doesn't always carry a full load. That's because, Arturo explains, a lot of people don't want to follow Sonny's rules: no alcohol or smoking ("How can we smoke and drink inside a temple of the Lord?" is Sonny's question.) Arturo shakes his head, "There are good people and bad people, all kinds of people on this bus."

Sonny tries to witness to some of the families on the bus, but not all are accepting. "Salvation doesn't mean anything to some of them," Arturo says. "They're very bitter and they have a bitterness towards God." Sonny, calm as ever, says his bus is a community service and that's enough for now.

For the most part the people on the prison bus don't talk much to each other. Instead, they stay in their family units, talking to a few friends in nearby seats. Two women, Joy and Maria (not their real names) are an exception. They met on this bus and are now close friends, joking and laughing together to help them forget the pain of having a husband and son in prison. "What would I do without Sonny?" Joy says. Maria grins and smacks her forehead. "What would I do without my V-8?" she mimics.

Maria lives in Eagle Pass and splits the trip to Huntsville by staying with Joy in San Antonio before catching Sonny's bus. Joy has visited her son ever since he was convicted of armed robbery five years ago. "It about killed me when (he) got in trouble. It's hard on wives and hard on mothers," she said, pulling nervously at her fingers. Last time after visiting her son she looked back and there he sat at a window. But all she could, was an arm waving a white handkerchief "for the longest time."

Joy worries about her son. Once she went to see him and he had been beaten up by the guards, she says. "It is so hard coming home after seeing them beat up like that or when they're sick I could die. I cried all the way home. There's nothing you can do. Your hands are tied."

At one point during the ride, Arturo gets into a conversation with a man who is riding the bus out of curiosity, another minister who works with alcoholics at a rescue mission downtown. (He brought with him little yellow pamphlets labeled "How to Get To Heaven From San Antonio" with a map on the front). Arturo asks him, "Do you believe terminal illness is demonically inspired by Satan." The man nods and solemnly says, "I really believe we're

Sonny and Diana share a quiet moment on the journey to visit her father

in the last days." Arturo replies "The Lord is going to come. Amen Hallelujah."

Soon the bus arrives at its first stop. It is 9 a.m. almost seven hours and 65 gallons of diesel fuel since Sonny's bus left San Antonio. This last stop, says Arturo as he pulls into the road leading up to the guard house is Ellis Unit, "for the losers." He shakes his head slowly. "That's where they have Death Row."

The bus stops at a barrier across the road and two women step out of the guard house to look over the bus and Sonny's list of visitors. One makes a phone call while the other talks with Arturo. A few steps beyond the gate is a white memorial stone ringed by a large wreath. It is dedicated to Wallace Pack and the prison farm manager who died with him both killed by an inmate who says he acted in self-defense. (He was acquitted in both deaths.)

The guards motion the bus through the gate and Sonny drives up to another guard house in front of a long, low spread of brick buildings. A chain-link fence topped with barbed wire separates the small house from the prison itself.

It is a clear, sunny day — a perfect day to be outdoors. Guards on horseback roam the fields outside the prison. Other men in white uniforms wash the warden's car and tend the green grass inside the barbed wire fence. These are trustees who because of good behavior are allowed more freedom than other inmates.

Diana comes out of the bathroom in back of the bus. She has changed out of her jeans into a frilly pink dress and her shiny black shoes. The long ride, sleeping on the seat of a jostling bus, all of this doesn't seem to have fazed her as she bounces down the bus stairs. She doesn't notice the chain-link fences or the guards up in the 25-foot watchtower staring down at the bus. All she wants to know is if she can take her teddy bear into the prison with her. She can't, says the guard. Sonny gives her some coins to buy Reynaldo soft drinks and that diverts her.

After she is cleared through the guard house Diana waits for the guards in the upper tower to trigger the gate's opening mechanism. Once through that gate she is inside a little metal cage caught between the "free world" as inmates call it and prison life. A group of trustees stop their gardening work to stare as she steps into the yard.

More guards inside the main building motion her into the small waiting room. About 20 other people are waiting for their names to be called and Diana spends her time staring at the other children. A steady drone of conversation comes from the main visiting room and it's hard to believe anyone can hear anyone else talk.

Visiting someone in prison is unlike being a prisoner. There is an immediate sense of losing control that at any time someone could give you a number and that would be it. It's not so much the scary metal doors clanging shut feeling as it is the awareness of a stifling web of bureaucracy. The heavy brick walls, the drab

CONTINUED

Sonny and his sidekick, Arturo Garza, behind the wheel, succumb to weariness during a rest break

colors, the metal on the windows, all of these reinforce the oppressive atmosphere. Everything and everyone has a place. Only during visits, Reynaldo says later, can inmates be themselves. They don't have to act tough or "wear masks" in front of their families.

Diana's name is called and she follows a guard who curtly tells her "number 24." She heads down a long row of chairs in front of a long wooden counter. People form an outer ring around the curved counter and inmates, all in white, are the inner ring. A thick glass wall, up to the ceiling, separates the two groups. Diana sees her father waving at her behind the glass and skips down to her seat. Women sit on either side of her. The young pregnant black woman on her right side has two little boys with her. They start to chase each other and she reaches down and gives one a quick, hard swat. The man on the other side watches mournfully, as the punishment is given out to the sons he can't touch.

Diana hops on the counter and presses her hand against the glass. On the other side, Reynaldo does the same thing. She giggles happily. The room vibrates with the sound of people talking, talking, trying to cram a month into two hours. Diana doesn't really spend much time talking to her father, and he doesn't expect it. He is just happy now that she recognizes him as her father. She draws on her paper and holds them up to the glass for him to see. Then she runs to buy

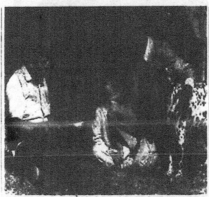

After the bus trip, Sonny, left, joins father and daughter for a longer reunion when Reynaldo is granted a four-day furlough.

him a soda, which the guard carries to Reynaldo.

Like Sonny, Reynaldo is a distinguished looking man of 49 with graying hair. His eyes are warm in his long, thin face, but he looks weary. Except when he's praising God. And Sonny.

"Sonny has been a real blessing to me. He has been a good example. He's my pastor and a man of God. He has done a lot of things I haven't seen other ministers do. He's the only one who has come over here and really tried to help us out," Reynaldo says with passion. Looking at Diana

through the glass, he adds "If it wasn't for him. I wouldn't be able to see my little girl."

Sonny is one of the few outside ministers allowed to hold chapel services in Texas prisons. His traveling prison ministry stems from his years in California, where he traveled with a chaplain who "testified" at state prisons. That made such an impression on him that he wanted to try the same thing when he returned to Texas. In a prison system that is much less progressive. At first prison officials were wary, and they allowed Sonny to council inmates only in the

prison warden's office. Soon, though, he started holding services in the prison chapels every month. He would stay in a motel for a week and travel to each prison farm around Huntsville.

While he was doing that, he started taking older women, "senior ladies," in his small pickup truck to visit their men in prison. During one of those trips he saw many more women, hitchhiking back from the prisons after visiting their sons. Once back in Huntsville they would wait until 9 p.m. that night to catch a bus back to San Antonio.

"It was real cold that night and I went to get coffee, but they didn't trust me to help them. I started crying before the Lord and praying for Him to do something to help them. He told me, 'You do it.'"

Sonny prayed and the Lord provided him with a van which he used to take a few people each month to Huntsville. From that van grew a fleet of buses. In each case, says Sonny, the Lord came through, changing $20,000 down payments into an offer of a free bus from a local bank in one case, bringing down the price of a 10-year old bus from $70,000 to $30,000 in another.

This is proof to Sonny that the Lord moves in strange and mysterious ways. But to the people who ride on his bus and the people he visits in prison, the Lord is getting a lot of help from Sonny.

Now he gets letters from inmates asking him to come testify. "If they

CENTERPIECE

want me to visit. I go. It's something real special for them," Sonny says, adding that the Ellis chapel, which seats 400, is usually filled during his three-hour services. It was in that chapel that Reynaldo says his life was changed. Reynaldo had been thinking a lot about God ever since his arrest. But Sonny encouraged him not just to think, but to act on his beliefs. He helped Reynaldo set up a prison Bible study for other inmates and Reynaldo got involved in the prison choir and Sunday school.

It wasn't the first time, though, that the two men's paths had crossed. Years before, while an addict in San Antonio, Reynaldo heard there was a man who helped junkies. Reynaldo went to visit Sonny's church. "I felt they really cared and there were these voices, 'Stay, Nayo, stay,' but I was scared. Right there, I think God was talking to me, but I rejected that." A year later, Reynaldo was arrested for selling heroin to an undercover agent, a "narco," and sent to prison for life.

Soon, a guard taps Reynaldo on the shoulder. It is time to go. The two hours are up. Diana waves to Reynaldo and behind the glass he returns the wave, trying not to show how sad he is. Back in the bus, Sonny waits for a woman who is still inside. Arturo is napping. Diana is running up and down the aisles, chatting with another little girl. And then everyone stops. There are shouts from within the barred windows, "Guard! Guard!" and a tremendous echoing,

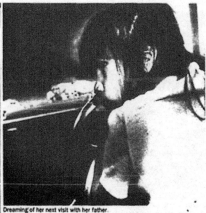

Dreaming of her next visit with her father.

hollow sound like hundreds of people banging metal against pipes. Arturo is laconic. "Somebody probably got stabbed," he says. "They're banging their metal cups against the bars to get the guards." The sound continues, surrounding the bus. No one in the guard house pays attention and soon the noise dies down.

On the ride home some people chat, others sleep. The mood is subdued. One woman sits alone, staring out the window. Suddenly there is a commotion in the back. A young woman with dark hair and tight jeans is slumped over in her seat. She lifts her head when Arturo goes to the back to see what's wrong. Her eyes are glazed and don't focus on him. "She took two pills, her young daughter tells Arturo. In a low voice he talks to the woman and then returns to the front of the bus. "She must have taken some downers after having a fight with her husband," Arturo says and shrugs. Except for that incident the ride home is uneventful. When the bus pulls up in front of Mario's 16 hours after the journey began, it is as dark as when it left.

Back at his church Sonny stands outside the chapel pointing out the buildings on his church grounds. "When we first came here in 1973 it was like a city dump all trees and swamp. We slept out in the open but we felt that God wanted us to work here and I felt God would supply it." The Lord will supply is Sonny's theme song. From dirt-cheap buses to raise money to build up his old crowd of drug-addict friends he grabbed off the streets. He held services out in the street amidst the trash and rubble. Pretty soon more and more people started coming, family members of addicts. Sonny's own brothers and sisters. With donations, Sonny bought nearly 30 more. He talked to the owner, a local banker who was asking $2,000 a lot. That man let Sonny have the lots for $500 each, payable at $20 a year.

That was the beginning of a long string of people who paved the way for Sonny's mission. (Sonny says the Lord did the roadwork, though.) A lumber company trusted him, an ex-junkie and ex-convict with credit to buy supplies to build a house. The

first priority was a building that would house a rehabilitation center and Bible program for the junkies. Those addicts brought their relatives so the next priority was a chapel.

No magnificent cathedral, the simple wooden chapel where Sonny holds services in English and Spanish is one of a series of mismatched buildings some worn down, some in the process of being fixed up. There is also a meeting hall where the 10 Bible students Sonny teaches meet, their faces intent, dog-eared Bibles firmly in hand.

Here, at Sonny's church, young drug addicts, people evicted from their homes, street wanderers, the spiritually dry, life's abandoned, all can find hope. And they repay him — and the Lord — with their faith and contributions. "We work with poor people. They're poor but they're grateful, so they give. They're not sleeping out on the streets, under cars no more, so they give and the Lord blesses what they give," Sonny says. What touches him most is finding food stamps in the collection plate.

Not long after the prison bus ride, with Sonny's help, Reynaldo is granted a four-day furlough, his first in seven years. Sonny has custody of him and Reynaldo stays at the church. Diana also comes to stay with her father, living with Sonny's family until her father returns to prison.

Reynaldo looks a little uncomfortable in his first suit of clothes after seven years. While he talks in the church dining hall, Diana devours a slice of watermelon, losing half of it to the floor. "I never pick up my voice at her. I believe she's been hurt enough." Reynaldo says as Diana rubs rind on her face and giggles. She then climbs up on his lap, and he hugs her. "If I can get out soon I'll make sure I show her all my love and affection," he says, adding that together "we can sing and play piano and preach. I want her to serve the Lord with me."

Diana's first reaction after seeing her father is, "Daddy, what man let you out of the jail?" That question pleases Reynaldo, for it means she recognizes him and that the prison visits are important not just to him but to her too. During the few days out of prison Reynaldo shows his daughter how to brush her teeth, how to pray. Outside behind the church he races with her letting her win "to encourage her to get better."

The hardest part about returning to prison after a brief taste of freedom is leaving Diana. "I'm going to miss her and I'm pretty sure she's going to miss me too, now that she's been with me a few days." It does seem in that brief time that the 6-year-old started to trust him more, to believe that this is her father. Standing outside on the night Sonny would drive him back to Huntsville, Reynaldo holds Diana close to him. "You see this little girl in my arms? I never held her in my arms. She's almost 7 years old and that's how long I've been in prison." As tears slide down his cheeks, Diana looks at him, puzzled. "Why are you crying?" Her father answers. "Because I love you."

Sarah Pattee is a staff writer in The Light's Living Today department.

JULY 8, 1984 SAN ANTONIO LIGHT/23

Summer Special

Beautiful Pools are Our Specialty!

- Many Designs to Choose from — Also Custom designing Available
- 15 Years of Satisfied Customers
- 100% Financing Available

We Can Construct an Almost Entirely
MAINTENANCE FREE
Gunite Swimming Pool for as little as
$9,995⁰⁰

Including Permits excavation, steel, gunite, plaster, cool deck, pump, filter, skimmer, cleaner, custom plumbing, wiring, light, tile, mastic...

Call for a Free Professional estimate

ANGIE POOLS OF AMERICA

5766 Evers   We also sell
(Wurzbach at Evers)   Rainbow   **681-1045**
Valley Park Shopping Center Products

The Bus Ministry

WHERE SAN ANTONIANS WORSHIP

RIGHT AT HOME: The Rev. Reynaldo "Sonny" Perales stands with his son, Sam, in front of a bus they used as a chapel and a home.

Former drug addict now has fix on God

PERALES: Pastor turns drug addicts to God

PASTOR/from E1

lies through the San Antonio for Christ Church at 341 Spaatz on the Southwest Side. Perales estimates "89½ percent" of his congregation is composed of former drug addicts and their families.

After his conversion, Perales attended the Latin American Bible Institute in La Puente, Calif. He returned to San Antonio to start a ministry to his old friends and associates in the drug trade.

Perales said he wanted to witness to the patrons of a notorious bar in the Palo Alto Heights neighborhood and came upon an empty lot with a "For Sale" sign nailed to a tree.

He persuaded the owner to reduce the $1,500 selling price to $750 — all the cash he had — and set up for God's business in a tent under the tree near an open field at the end of Spaatz Street.

Perales obtained slightly fancier quarters when someone gave him an old bus, which he converted into a chapel and home for him, his wife and two children. The old bus still sits behind the 400-seat sanctuary where the congregation now worships.

With donations and a lot of volunteer labor by church members, Perales has added a home, a classroom building and three old military barracks used to house recovering addicts or alcoholics.

But buses still are an important

San Antonio for Christ Church

part of the church's ministry.

Twice a month, the church sponsors two or three buses that carry people with family members in prison to the Texas Department of Corrections in Huntsville. With bus and taxi fare to the prison units costing $75 or more, Perales' $20 fare makes it possible for many people to see a husband, son, father or brother to whom they otherwise might not talk for years. For people with little income, even the $20 will be waived.

The bus trips start at 2 a.m. Saturday and last for 18 hours with travel time to and from Huntsville and trips back and forth among the prison units to drop off and pick up the visitors.

Perales said the bus ministry has been an important first contact with many people who have become active in the church.

Perales believes faith in God is the only way an addict can get off drugs permanently.

"You can get somebody to leave heroin for a few months, but (without God) you can't get it out of his mind," Perales said. "When God gets you free, you'll feel like you've never been a drug addict."

Caesar Garcia, Bexar County chief probation officer, said his office has referred probationers to Perales.

Garcia said Perales succeeds with many addicts because he is "streetwise" from his own experience, but not all drug users will respond to religious motivation.

"I have seen people who have gone through many programs, who get a religious motivation and decide on their own to get off heroin," Garcia said. "It all depends on the individual. The religious approach is more likely to work with the older addict, who is tired of roaming the streets."

Perales thinks his drug program is threatened by new state licensing requirements for all drug and alcohol treatment centers. He said the rules would require his counselors to be state-approved and would prevent him from requiring daily Bible reading.

"They say we're not qualified to counsel with drug addicts," Perales scoffed. "We're not qualified to work with them and we've got hundreds, maybe thousands, who have been rehabilitated?"

But Lucille Gray, licensing director for the Texas Commission on Alcoholism and Drug Abuse, said many church-related groups have misunderstood the licensing requirements.

Gray said Bible studies could be part of a drug program as long as clients were informed of that requirement before admission.

She said the state would not try to license such things as faith healing, but a structured program would need at least one certified drug-abuse counselor to inform patients about the medical aspects of addiction.

"We don't want to prohibit people from being in contact with ministers, but we need a structured program with counseling on a one-to-one basis about the disease process," Gray said.

VaRiety is the spice of life. Find it in the comic pages of the **San Antonio Light**

CHAPTER FOURTEEN

Restoration Testimonies

> *"And they overcame him by the blood of the Lamb and **by the word of their testimony...** Revelation 12:10*

EVER SINCE I WAS A LITTLE GIRL, I felt a deep hurt and pain inside my heart. I felt a terrible emptiness and profound loneliness that I could not understand. I did not have any love inside of me nor had I ever felt it. I was always sad. My parents did not know Jesus. We were raised in a dark world and very, very poor. As a child, I remember feeling a lot of hurt and anguish; fear controlled me most of the time. I could not understand it. Why were we so poor? My father was an alcoholic and our family kept growing and growing. Poverty shattered my life as a little girl. I attended church but it was just a religious act for us, nothing ever changed. In 1964, I dropped out of high school. I went looking for a way out of the type of life I knew but little did I realize where I would end up.

I became a drug addict at age sixteen and lost control of my life entirely. Even though fear had always had a strong grasp of me, I started living in empty houses and cars and when night arrived, I would be searching for my next place to sleep. This led me to a life of stealing, dealing and prostitution. I was arrested several times for possession of drugs.

I was bitter, hopeless and miserable in complete bondage to drugs and I was a slave to sin. I was angry and I did not know how to change. I tried every way I knew how to live; good, bad, up, down and nothing work. I was sent to psychiatrists, counselors and psychologists. I was close to death many times in my darkest hours as I roamed the cold streets, the cemeteries, helpless and hopeless. No one could ever imagine how desperate I felt. I went through the worse kinds of degradation. I was beaten up, I went in and out of jail and in and out of rehabilitation centers but I always went back to drugs. I wanted to die. I was raped many times, beaten up and left for dead on several occasions. Most of the time I walked around in a daze, my brain was lethargic. I don't even know how I was even walking most of the time. I could not make any decisions. I was lost and blind. There was no way out for me, it seemed. I looked and searched in bars, in the streets of the good neighborhoods and in the bad neighborhoods. I even went to Mexico running from my terrible and painful life. I got involved with Fred Carrasco, thinking that if I had all the money and drugs I wanted, I would be happy forever. That was a lie from the devil; Satan, that great deceiver. There were days I did not want to wake up at all because very day it seemed like something ugly and terrible would happen to me.

I could not trust anyone. Many times I would cry out to God for help. I couldn't take it anymore. I felt I had to yell out loud, really loud, because God was in heaven and He could not hear me. I was looking for peace. One day someone told me about Jesus. They said that Jesus was calling for me. They quoted the scripture found in Matthew 11:28, "Come unto me, all ye that labor and are heavy laden and I will give you rest." They told me about Jesus and how He died on the cross of Calvary for my sins and that He loved me. Me! Angie! Jesus loves me! He wants to set me free! Wow, those were sweet words to me.

They said, "Jesus loves you Angie. He wants to come into your life and wants you to trust Him. He cares for you and He wants to make you whole. He is loving and merciful. Jesus loves you and He can change your life."

I believed those words and the glory of Jesus transformed me and gave me a new life. I can now love again. I am not afraid anymore and I can trust again. I have hope, real hope, eternal hope. I am clean. I am no longer addicted to drugs and I have peace, sweet, wonderful peace in my life. Jesus Christ has dressed me in white linen. He has given me His righteousness. I praise my Lord and Savior. I am serving our Lord God and have been for a long time now. I am happily married and have a beautiful family. I have a good home and I attend church regularly. Beloved, there is hope for you. Jesus can give you a new life. He can make you whole.

Matthew 9:22 "For she said within herself, if I but touch His garment, I shall be made whole. But Jesus turning and seeing her said, daughter, be of good cheer; thy faith hath made thee whole. And the woman was made whole from that very hour."

Angie Flores
Member of San Antonio for Christ Church

In those days, my wife Mary knew the Lord; she attended San Antonio for Christ Church regularly. She had asked me for permission to go to that church and I said yes because I was not serving God and I knew it would give me more time to do the things that I wanted to do without my wife around. She asked my permission to attend their Bible Institute and I liked that idea even better because, again, it would give me some more free time. She would be gone to the classes and she would either take the kids with her or arrange for someone else to watch them while she was in class. That gave me lots of free time to do my drinking and hang out with my unsaved friends.

One evening, I was hanging out at a neighborhood ice house,

drinking with the guys and dancing with the girls. I never went in for the drugs, I just liked the good times. I had parked my truck out in front and I was just having a good time when Mary blew the horn of my car, I recognized it right away. I thought she had seen my parked truck so I went out to speak to my wife. I asked her if she had stopped because she saw my truck and she said no, that she had been visiting her mother but at the same time she had been praying for me and that the Lord had led her to me. This happened three or four times. Mary said she would pray to God to guide her to where I was so that she could warn me to be careful of impending danger.

One day, my friends invited me to an ice house outside of town by Nacogdoches Road and Hiway 1604. I thought for sure she would not find me there because it was so far out of town and I had never been there before. I even had a hard time finding the place myself. The thought crossed my mind, after I arrived, that this place was so far that she would never even think about coming out this far. Well, about 11pm, we were having a good time, drinking and dancing when I heard the horn of my car. I thought, "It can't be, this is too far." But I thought I'd better go check anyway so I walked out to see if my wife was there." When I saw her something strange and powerful came over me and I felt like I had been set free. It was like I had been tied somehow and now the chains had fallen off of me. Like I had somehow been blind but now I could see clearly. I knew this was a supernatural act from God. Only God's power could have guided Mary to me and filled me with such a strange and joyful feeling. I remember it like it was just yesterday. I went to her and asked her, "What are you doing here?" Mary said, "Didn't I tell you, it was God's Holy Spirit that has led me here to you. I'm not sure why but I think we should leave." I said to Mary, "Wait right here, let me go back to get my change on the table and then I'll follow you with my truck. Mary was driving our car. I felt this strong force again, a very strong feeling stopping me from going inside so instead I turned around, got into my truck right away and Mary and I went home. Later we would find out that there was a shooting that night and that I could have been killed had I gone back inside.

1 Corinthians 1:18 "For the message of the cross is foolishness to those who are perishing but to us who are being saved, it is the power of God."

I knew that it was God who was calling me. I knew this was power from above, a supernatural power bigger than me, bigger than the good times that I wanted. This was on a Saturday night and it was late when we got back home but early Sunday morning, I got up and started getting dressed. Mary asked me, "Where are you going?" I shocked her and my whole family when I replied, "I am going to church with you." That day, in late October, 1978, I accepted the Lord Jesus Christ as my Savior and Lord. After that I realized that what I had been missing all my life was the presence of God in my life. I have been at San Antonio for Christ Church ever since. It's been 21 years and I was given a new life that unforgettable night. My God is a powerful and loving God.

When I share the word of God and witness about the things that Jesus has done in my life, I tell all who will listen to me that Jesus is the answer. I loved to drink and dance, I loved the world and all it had to offer but I know now that Jesus can set you free and fill you with such joy, love and peace that the world can never give you. I am not of this world. I am just a stranger in this land. Jesus has changed me and has made me a new creature.

2 Corinthians 5:17 "Therefore, if anyone is in Christ, he is a new creation, the old has gone, the new has come."

Whatever your problem may be, I know God can help you. He gave me my freedom and He can give it to you. On my job, I am a supervisor and work with many unsaved people. Their manners and lifestyles are completely opposite mine now. Some knew me before I was changed and transformed by God and they no longer understand me. We don't speak the same language but they respect me and obey me when I give them an order. The Lord has given me compassion for them. I love them and pray for them. The Lord Jesus is not slow in keeping His promise as some understand slowness. He is patient with us, not wanting anyone to perish but everyone to come to repentance. I give all the glory and honor to

God for what He had done in my life. I will never forget the night He set me free.

Albert DeLaCruz
Member of San Antonio for Christ Church

I remember I could not get along with my Mother. There were ten children in my family and eight were half brothers and sisters. My brother was fourteen years old and it was obvious that he was her favorite. I was thirteen years old when I first left home because I had problems getting along or perhaps I just didn't feel that I was wanted at home. I started smoking cigarettes, then I graduated to marijuana, crack, cocaine, heroin and along the way I sniffed spray and smoked hash. I also sniffed "rush", which is highly potent and goes directly to the brain. In school, I would sniff lighter fluid that was poured onto a handkerchief. It would make me high right away, it also goes directly to the brain and it is very inexpensive so many of the kids do it while in school.

At fifteen, I had already fathered a baby and I was selling drugs. At the time, I lived in San Carlos and Chupaderas, Mexico. Drugs were my life by my early teens and they drove me deeper into the drug world. I didn't care if people got hooked on the drugs I sold them and those that did not pay; I would beat up really bad. What I believe I was lacking in my family was love and acceptance so I ran away from home. That only led me to a life of crime and drug abuse.

My father had been a King Pin and he had taken us to bars when we were very young. My brothers and I heard gun shots and saw drug dealings and drug use at a very young age. My half-brothers are all in the penitentiary now.

What I went through personally, my wife and children also went through because I was a heavy drug user and also a pusher. I hurt my family severely. I loved my children but I was in bondage to a rough lifestyle. I married Joann and her father was also a drug user and had been on heroin most of his life. Joann had gone through all this kind of hell, just like me, even before we married.

On August of 1996, I was busted with drugs but quickly came out on bond. I continued with the same lifestyle and started dealing again. I missed my father-in-law so I looked him up and found that he was now living in San Antonio, Texas and that he was living at The San Antonio for Christ Rehabilitation Home. I wanted nothing to do with a church. I just wanted to visit my father-in-law. It was New Year's Eve and we were having a party at my house that night but my wife and I wanted to see him so we went to the Home.

As soon as he saw me, he hugged me and told me that he loved me and that I should quit drugs. I still remember the hug he gave me that night; it was different from before. He seemed to be a changed man. He introduced me to Brother Salome, one of the leaders at the Home. We were invited to come in to their New Year's Eve service they were having that night at their church. My wife looked at me and she knew right away that I did not want to go in. My father-in-law took us in and sat us at the very front of the church where all the men from the Home sit. My wife sat next to her dad and she hugged and kissed him. It was a family reunion for us.

The devil, the Father of Lies, started working on me right away and I almost walked outside when I heard one of the men give his testimony. Part of his testimony was that he used to break into houses to steal things to support his drug habit. During one of his break-ins, he discovered that the owner was in the house and in the struggle; his eye was injured very badly. God had healed his eye and now he could see clearly. This man seemed overly joyful and a healing like that was hard to believe. I was getting fidgety and my mother-in-law was concerned that I might walk out but then Brother Villegas started sharing his testimony so I did not get up to leave. Every time I thought I would leave, some strange and powerful force kept me down in my seat. This time, during the testimony, I felt like crying. That was a very strange feeling for me.

I had never seen my in-laws hold each other's hands. I had

never seen them look like that at each other before. They were so different, completely different people, and they were treating each other with such love and care. We had to leave because our children were at their grandmother's and we had the party at my house going on that night. When we got back to my house, I saw the world as it really is. I saw the drinking, the madness, the wildness and I felt like a stranger in my own home. In just those brief few minutes sitting at The San Antonio for Christ Church, I was changed. I was now a different man inside.

I had a big drug deal going down in the next few days but when I saw the drug world through new eyes, I knew I did not want that kind of life any more. I told my wife that I wanted to go back to church that same night because I knew the church was going to be open all night because it was New Year's Eve and the "Noche de Vigilia". For some reason, we couldn't get back to church that night and our party went on but I was feeling very uncomfortable. The beer did not taste the same anymore. I was offered drugs but I did not want them anymore. What was the matter with me? My mind was back at The San Antonio for Christ Church. God had spoken to my spirit and changed my heart. Now I wanted the kind of life that I saw there instead of the kind of life that I had.

My case was pending for the 1996 charge and they wanted to give me twenty years. I started coming to church and Pastor Sonny Perales had many questions and gave me great godly counseling. He told me to be sincere with God and that God would help me. He said I should keep coming to church, focus on serving God and do not worry about the case. But I was new so I doubted and worried. I remember that the Sunday before my court date, Pastor Sonny asked the whole church to pray for me and gave me a hug and told me that Jesus loves me. The Pastor was crying and he said, "Jesus is going to go with you and He is going to use you and bring you back to us. Jesus is your lawyer." I felt their love and wondered why Pastor Sonny had tears in his eyes. I thought to myself, "He doesn't even know me that well, why would he be crying for me?"

When I went to court, the devil asked me, "Where is your Pastor?" I had asked the Pastor to go with me but his response was, "I am just a man, I'm a nobody, but the One who can help you is going with you and that is Jesus."

I said my goodbyes to my wife, gave her all my belongings and told her to keep going to church. Everybody in court that day was getting five to ten years. DWI's were getting five years and my charges were much more serious than that. Thankfully, it was my first offense and I had worked for the County so they took that into consideration. Because they did not catch me with the money, they dropped one case against me but still wanted to give me ten years for the drug possession. The devil kept messing with my mind. He kept telling me, "There is no Jesus and the church and the Pastor don't care about you." Then I looked around and saw my wife, Joann, in the corner of the courtroom and she was hugging her Bible. I was encouraged and I seemed to receive strength knowing that I was not alone and that Jesus was in the courtroom with us.

The Judge was growing tired; it had been a very long day. I was the last one getting prosecuted that day. She took a break and while I waited I talked with my wife. Then my lawyer asked the Prosecutor to give me a break. The Prosecutor got so upset that she banged her fist on the table and told my lawyer that if he kept asking, she was going to ask the Judge to give me even more time.

That Prosecutor then received a call and left the courtroom and another Prosecutor took her place. A few minutes after that first Prosecutor left the room, the Judge returned and I was given eight years' probation. No jail time, just probation. I was so relieved and so grateful to Jesus for advocating my case.

God is a God of second changes. I could never thank Him enough. He has given me a new life and a new family. I am in charge of the order in church services now and I keep track of the kitchen at San Antonio for Christ Rehabilitation Home and Church. I help my Pastor in whatever I can and I take the men to pass out Christian tracts and witness to people. I am constantly ministering to the lost and giving others my testimony. I want everyone to know what I know and that is that Jesus saves, heals and transforms lives. I was dead but now I am alive! Thank you Jesus Christ!

Mike Aviles
Member of San Antonio of Christ

"For I am not ashamed of the gospel of Christ, for it is the power of God to salvation for everyone who believes, for the Jew first and also for the Greek. For in it the **righteousness of God is revealed from faith** to faith, as it is written, "The just shall live by faith." Romans 1:16 & 17

CHAPTER FIFTEEN

Lydia

> "Those who sow in tears **shall reap in joy.** He who continually goes forth weeping, bearing seed for sowing, **shall doubtless come again with rejoicing,** bringing his sheaves with him." Psalm 126:5 & 6

I grew up on the west side of San Antonio, Texas around the Tampico Street area. Like most Hispanic families of that time, ours was big; there were twelve of us. Two have since died so now we are ten in the family. I grew up with constant drinking and fighting in our family but no matter what was said or done, we always asked each other for forgiveness. I came from very humble beginnings and at the age of twelve, I went to a Pentecostal church service and learned about answered prayer. I remember praying for my father to stop drinking and thankfully, he did. I was still a child but God was already teaching me His ways. My father abandoned the family and divorced my mother so we grew up very, very poor and went through many difficult trials.

When I was fifteen, I yearned to get married to a Christian man. I did not want him to smoke or drink. I wanted to have a different life than what I had experienced with my parents. Although I tried, it seemed that the Christian boys never even gave me a second look. Now I believe that this was from God because one year later, I would meet and marry Sonny.

I was working at a restaurant as a waitress and Sonny came in for the very first time. When our eyes met, I felt something in my heart but at the same time, I felt almost an apprehension, something gripped at my heart. It may have been love at first sight, I don't know, but I know something inside of me connected with Sonny at that very moment. I did not see him again until much later when my father rented a house from Sonny's parents and Sonny lived next door to us. About three months after we moved next door to Sonny and his parents, Sonny asked me for a date. It turned out to be a three-day date and after that, we married.

Sonny came from a Christian home but he did not want anything to do with God. In the first year of our marriage, I received Jesus Christ as my Lord and Savior. I would go to church with my mother-in-law regularly and she was a tremendous blessing to me. God used her for my spiritual growth and she taught me to ask for petitions from God and so I would ask for Sonny's salvation at each church service. The Holy Spirit would somehow bring Sonny to church because during the service, Sonny would just show up in church.

During this time of my marriage, I saw shootings, my life was threatened several times, my husband was a drug addict and very violent, I was afraid of him most of the time because he would beat me for almost any reason. Through all these violent and turbulent years, I loved him and God gave me the strength to go on. I knew one day God would save him. I got in the habit of praying for my husband for at least one hour per day. I would get up from my prayer hour and my legs would be numb and weak, I would sometimes fall or trip while trying to get up. I never strayed from the married although it was very difficult because I feared God and I wanted to stay faithful to my God.

One day, because I did not feel he paid any real attention to me, I tried to make him jealous and desire me by changing the color of my hair. He was out of town, in Dallas, at the time and when he came home, my hair was blonde. He took one look at me and became furious, grabbed me and took me out to the woods. I thought he was going to beat me but little did I realize that his intentions were to kill me. As he was yelling at me, throwing me to the ground, he pulled out a gun, I clearly remembered a church sermon that spoke about claiming "the blood of Jesus" for your rescue. Three times I screamed, "the blood of Jesus", "the blood of Jesus", "the blood of Jesus" out loud as he was pointing the gun at me. During this time, I could hear an audible gorilla sound, much like King Kong. There was a large shadow behind Sonny while he was yelling at me and I was crouching down. All of a sudden, something bit Sonny on the ankle. It turned out to be a snake, a non-venomous snake but it was enough to stop Sonny from killing me. He had torn all the clothes off of me in his rage so he grabbed me, pushed me into the car and took me to a hotel where I called my sister-in-law, Frances, to please bring me some clothes. It was a Sunday morning and she and her family were on their way to church. She came by the hotel room and brought me a blouse and skirt to put on and by that time, Sonny was calmed down and tending to his snake bite.

Another time in which, looking back now, I see the hand of God protecting us and healing our traumas is when Sonny and I were living in Dallas. I was pregnant with our first son; Jesse, and Sonny had built up a large network of drug dealing activity between Dallas, San Antonio and Mexico. He had become well known in the underworld and the shipment of drugs became larger and larger. With each drug shipment, the transactions become even more dangerous. This particular occasion found me alone in our apartment and Sonny had taken his right-hand man to work out the details of a shipment whose drop off location had been changed at the last minute. He was suspicious that someone was trying to steal the drugs. So he left me a gun and told me not to open the door to anyone and to shoot if I had to, to protect myself. He gave me five hundred dollars and asked me to hide it. I tucked it into my bra. I was seven months pregnant at the time.

Not long after Sonny left, two gentlemen dressed as police officers came knocking at our door. I was very suspicious but because they identified themselves as police officers and were dressed that way, I opened the door to them and they asked to see Sonny. When I told them that he was not at home, one of them stayed with me and the other went into the bedrooms to look for him and then went downstairs into the parking lot to search further. I really thought that they were policeman but as we waited in the living room, the man standing next to me said, "You're pregnant?" and reached over and placed his hand on my stomach. When he did that, I realized right away that he was not a policeman. Maybe he thought I was hiding drugs under my clothes, I don't know for sure but I became very fearful and began thinking of what I could do to get away and also to warn Sonny should he return. I slowly walked over to the large window overlooking the parking lot and noticed a large piece of iron with bolts, screws and washers attached to it and I thought that I would pick it up and throw it through the window or out the opened door to warn Sonny should I hear him approaching the apartment. I could feel my blood pressure rising, I was afraid they would harm me or my baby if they did not find Sonny or any drugs in our apartment so my mind was racing to think of how to escape from them, if I had to.

As I sat by the window, I thought I heard Sonny's truck driving up and then I heard steps coming up the stairwell and in my anxious state, I assumed it was Sonny. I was focused on warning him to prevent these men from killing him so I started to scream at the top of my lungs. The man that walked through the door was not Sonny but the other person dressed like a policeman. They were so mad at me that they grabbed me and forcibly began taking me downstairs. I believe they were going to kidnap me and blackmail Sonny into giving them the drugs or money for my return. I was trying to pull away from them when I fell down. I was wearing new sandals and one of them got caught on the steps, which caused me to fall. I was screaming for help as they were dragging me to their vehicle. Some of the neighbors heard me and began coming out of their apartments to see what was happening. The men got scared with all the on-lookers and one of them screamed;

"Los Perros" (the dogs) and they fled and left me on the stairwell.

I was so scared and baby Jesse started jumping and turning inside my womb. The baby felt all my fears. He was jumping and kicking in my womb because of my high anxiety, he felt everything I felt. Sonny got home with his friend Andres. I told them what had happened and they went to Andres' house to get some guns and when they arrived, they found those same two men ransacking that house to try and find drugs or money to steal.

I was very sick for the rest of my pregnancy and Jesse was born a month early. He had wrapped himself up in the umbilical cord three times due to my emotional and fearful state. He felt all my pain and when I went into labor, I was in hard labor for three days. I laid in the hospital in severe pain and I felt like I was in a long dark tunnel and I kept going out of conciseness and the nurse would slap me on the face to bring me back. I felt like I was going into a much needed sleep out of sheer exhaustion. Finally, Jesse was born. He had been choking all night on the cords and he struggled to get out, he was so tired and blue all over. I thank God he survived this ordeal.

When my son grew up, there were many fearful and negative emotions and scars evident in his life. We always called him, "boy". Recently, I obeyed God and started to bind all those memories and emotions Jesse still had churning inside of him. John the Baptist leaped for JOY but my Jesse leaped for FEAR. But now our son is free by the power of Jesus Christ and his face shines with peace. He has been healed and attended Latin American Bible Institute. Jesse wants to minister to Pastor's kids as he can relate to that particular life and the demands and pressures it brings on young people.

Because of God's grace, I was not killed that terrible day when those men came looking for Sonny and sadly, those men were later killed that week in another drug break-in.

After ten long and very difficult years of marriage, one day Sonny's brother, Joel, asked him to take him to La Puente, California and it was there that God touched Sonny's life and changed him forever. I was about to divorce Sonny but when

I saw the miraculous transformation that God had done in his life, I stayed and our marriage was healed and transformed so completely, it was as if I was married to a new man. He spoke so differently; his thoughts and actions were unrecognizable to me. Indeed, Sonny had become a new creature by the power of Jesus Christ.

I followed him to California and we lived there for four years where Sonny attended Latin American Bible Institute in La Puente, California and received his degree in Christian Theology.

God called Sonny back to San Antonio in 1973 and gave him a large piece of land and so the beginning of a home for drug addicts in the Palo Alto area of the south side of San Antonio began. This was the beginning of San Antonio for Christ. We were living in an old 1938 Greyhound bus for several years. Sonny and I, three children, I was pregnant during that period and we had several drug addicts that had accepted Jesus Christ as their Savior living with us while Sonny ministered to their needs and they broke their drug habits. Working with drug addicts was not an easy task. Coming mostly from the streets, there is a real toughness about them. I felt pressure all the time; there was never any privacy for the children or myself. We spent so much time with the men that our children many times felt neglected since the demands of the Rehabilitation Home were so high. I would pray and cry to the Lord that He would give me the strength to go on. He showed me a vision that we would be prospered in the future. I believed it and waited on it and today we are greatly prospered by the grace of God. Many, many families have been saved, restored and reconciled by the power of God and through this ministry. I thank God for that.

San Antonio for Christ Ministries has grown and many ministers have graduated from the San Antonio for Christ Bible Institute. What God gave to Sonny; he has given back many times over. The ministry now has many buildings and God has given me a large home, no more living in a tight bus for us! The glory of God has manifested in my life in many wonderful ways. I did not know how to read and write but now I teach women bible studies, how to dress properly and be good wives. I teach them how to pray for their husbands and families, how to serve God and how to put Him first. Through the ministry of intercession, many prayers have been answered, especially in my own children's lives. God has used me in counseling others, street ministry, housing projects, supporting my husband in his ministry and calling and winning many beautiful souls for the kingdom of God.

My vision for the future is the preparation of my own children and the youth for the ministry of God. The power of the Lord is seen in our church worship services with many healings and miracles taking place. I am privileged to be a part of this ministry. Even though I went through ten years of a hard marriage, those tears have reaped true joy in my life and God has granted the desire of my heart in giving me a Christian husband. We have been happily married for over fifty-five years. As a matter of fact, God has given me so much more than I expected. He has also given me a Pastor, an Evangelist, a Teacher, an Administrator, a Bible Institute Director, a Counselor and Businessman as well as a godly and loving husband. I love my husband very much and I thank God for the tremendous blessing he has been to me personally, our own children, grandchildren and so many other families and individuals who Sonny has ministered to.

I was in love with God and I put up with the difficult life I had because I knew Jesus had suffered even more. I took it because I loved God and He gave me the strength, hope and courage to continue in my marriage. I give God all the credit for transforming Sonny and our marriage to bring him honor and glory and use us to bring many people to the gospel truth and to receive the gift of salvation. It took a miraculous and godly intervention to break the chains of addiction, violence, anger and ungodly mindsets that controlled Sonny for so long and to create a loving, godly and righteous person whose character is full of godly mercy, forgiveness and unconditional love. Jesus Christ is the only answer if you need a miracle, if you need to break your chains and set yourself or a loved one free. Reach out to Jesus; he is just a prayer away.

If you are ready to accept Jesus Christ as your Lord and Savior, prayer this short prayer:

"Jesus, please forgive me. I repent of my disobedience and of trying to do things my own way. I accept your way, your truth, and your gift of salvation. Cleanse me of all unrighteousness and make me a new creation. Wipe my sins away and give me a clean slate. Break the chains that have kept me a prisoner and heal and restore me to accomplish all that I was created to do. I receive you as my Lord and Savior and I will obey and follow you all the days of my life. I thank you and worship you to as the Son of God and the one true, living God. Amen"

If you have just prayed that prayer, we welcome you to the family of God. You are now a child of the living God, the King of kings and the Lord of lords. You now belong to the Kingdom of Light. You are free from your old habits, strongholds and past sins. Rejoice for God has made you free! You have been baptized with the love of God and you are being filled with incredible joy, peace and a good future. Began to read the Word of God every day and communicate with God daily so that He can reveal your destiny and godly purpose and lead you to your next steps. Find a good Bible-believing church to attend regularly and get connected with people of faith that are filled with the love and character of God. Connect with your new family members and draw closer and closer to God by reading and hearing His Word on a daily basis.

May the peace of God and the abundant blessings and prosperity of Christ be upon you and all those connected to you.

"Therefore, if anyone is in Christ, **he is a new creation all things have passed away and behold all things have become new."** 2 Corinthians 5:17

CHAPTER SIXTEEN

A Visual Timeline of Transformation and Miracles

1972: Sonny graduates from Latin American Bible Institute in La Puente, California

1973: Clearing out the first lots donated for the San Antonio for Christ Rehabilitation Home.

A Visual Timeline of Transformation and Miracles

1973: Having Bible Studies under the tree.

1973: The Bus where Sonny and his family lived.

1973: Faithful volunteers came to clear the land.

1976: San Antonio for Christ Church

A Visual Timeline of Transformation and Miracles   187

1976: A San Antonio for Christ Church social.

1976 – Water Baptism at SAFC

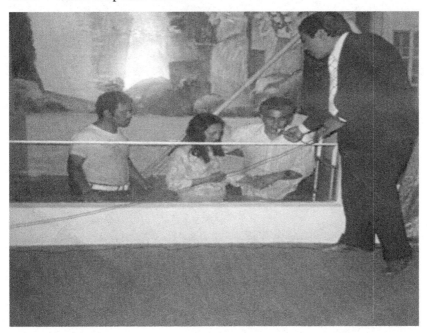

1978: The children and teens of San Antonio for Christ Church meeting under the trees each Sunday.

A Visual Timeline of Transformation and Miracles

1978 – Building the Parking Lot

1980: A Tent Revival on the grounds of San Antonio for Christ. Many souls came to Christ, many healings, restorations and deliverances.

1980: A Tent Revival *(continued)*

1980: A Tent Revival *(continued)*

A Visual Timeline of Transformation and Miracles

1980: A Men's Retreat from the Rehab Home

1982: Resurrection Sunday – Baptizing new members

1983: The altar is full after a powerful move of the Holy Spirit at San Antonio for Christ Church.

1983-1986 Day Care Center at SAFC

A Visual Timeline of Transformation and Miracles 193

1988-89: SAFC Graduating Bible Class

1988-89: SAFC Graduating Bible Class *(continued)*

1990 – Thanksgiving Harvest at SAFC

1993: A Miracle: Valentine Juerta is healed from severe burns.

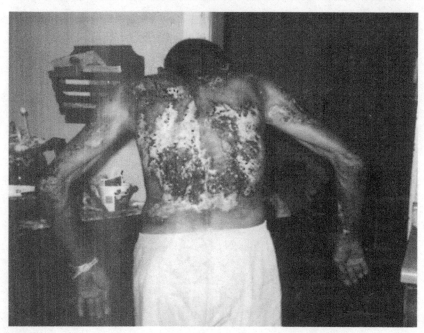

A Visual Timeline of Transformation and Miracles   195

1995: Baby Dedication

1997: Family Wedding at SAFC

1997: Pastors Sonny and Lydia Perales

1998: Pastors Sonny and Lydia Perales

A Visual Timeline of Transformation and Miracles

1999: Pastor Sonny and son, Michael

2000: Sonny & Lydia's 40th Wedding Anniversary

2000: 40th Wedding Anniversary with Family

2000: 40th Wedding Anniversary with eldest son, Jesse and Joe and Frances Rodriguez

A Visual Timeline of Transformation and Miracles 199

2001: Youth Conference

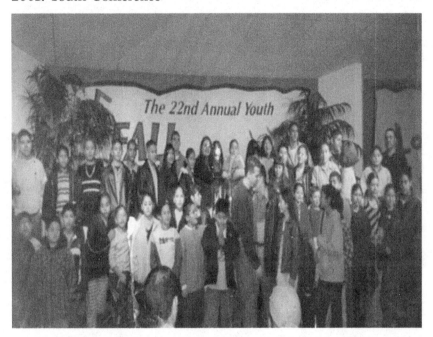

2001: Roasting a Pig and singing hymns

2002: Ladies Retreat

2003: Ladies Conference

A Visual Timeline of Transformation and Miracles 201

2004: Ladies Conference

2004: Vacation Bible School at SAFC

2004: Pastors Sonny and Lydia Perales

2005: Ladies Retreat

2006: Church Retreat

2007: Thanksgiving with the Perales Family

2015: Sam's Birthday (January 18th) The Perales siblings, from left, Sam, Jesse, Elizabeth and Michael

2015: Christmas with the Perales Family

Dedication

I would like to dedicate this book to my Lord, Jesus Christ, without whom I would not be the man I am today. It was Jesus who completely transformed my life from a life of drugs, violence and hopelessness to a life filled with miracles, love and more than I could have ever imagined. He truly has been faithful to His word and His promises and I can recommend His love and His plan of salvation to every person. I dedicated my life to Him the day I accepted Him as my Lord and Savior. Now I dedicate this book to Him and I pray that every reader would accept Him into their heart. When you do, your life will change forever and for the better. May God bless you, may His face shine upon you and may you enjoy the prosperity of God. To Lydia, I thank you for all your love and support. To my children, Jesse, Michael, Elizabeth and Sammy, I thank you and declare blessings over your lives, my grandchildren and many generations beyond. I love you all forever.

Acknowledgements

I would like to acknowledge my constant companion and loving wife, Lydia. She did not always have an easy life with me in the early years but she was always faithful to me and to God. She loves God with all her heart and she has been a loving help mate to me in the work that God called us to do.

I would like to acknowledge my sons and daughter in this ministry. They have been a true help to me at San Antonio For Christ and in our family. Thank you for blessing my life with so much love.

I would like to acknowledge all those individuals that have helped me at San Antonio For Christ and throughout the years of building it up. There are too many of you to name individually but you know who you are. Without your help, I could not have accomplished all that has been accomplished. Thank you for your support, faithfulness and constant prayers.

To God be the glory!